FULL THROTTLE

Scott "Beef "Bidwell

PAGE PUBLISHING
Conneaut Lake, PA

First originally published by Page Publishing 2024

ISBN 979-8-89315-863-2 (pbk)
ISBN 979-8-89315-879-3 (digital)

Printed in the United States of America

DEDICATION

I DEDICATE THIS **book to my grandfather, "Slick". I
believe you learn through other people, and that
man taught me a lot about life.**

THIS BOOK CONTAINS elements of tragedy, fear, excitement, heart-ache, guts, happiness, determination, victory, and a little sex. I hope you enjoy this shit because I did.

NIGHT BEFORE

September 18, 1987

ON A FRIDAY night, most boys would be out looking for girls, but not these guys. Ed and I were getting dressed up to go looking for our favorite dates, good old white-tailed deer. We slid into our camo, then headed down the road to one of Ed's favorite hotspots.

Ed was one of my best friends. We liked all the same activities, from sports to fishing, hunting, and chasing girls. Every time we got together, we found our way to the great outdoors in some fashion. I was the guy who started archery hunting at age twelve. One of my neighbors used to shoot his bow every night, and then I would go down and bullshit about bow hunting with him while he practiced. He let me shoot his bow every time I showed up, and then I obviously fell in love with the sport. I told dad I wanted a bow to hunt, and then he said, "You don't want a bow. Didn't you see how skinny the Indians were?" Dad never bowhunted growing up, so it was foreign to him, as he didn't really know anything about hunting that way. I was a stubborn kid, so once I put my mind to something, I was going to do it and do it well. All I had to do was persuade Dad to give me a chance.

The persistence paid off as Dad took me to Cooper's archery shop to look for a bow of my own. He got me a Darton compound bow, and then we headed to a farmer friend of Dad's to get some hay bales to shoot into, but not even close to the targets we were shooting at today. I was ready, my own bow, my own target, and so excited I felt like a bomb ready to explode. I practiced daily and then got to the point where I could put a nice group of arrows together each time I shot, but I found out Scottie boy wasn't the master of his archery domain he thought he was. Deers don't follow a script or go to the opening you thought had covered. They don't stop when you're ready or come in the direction you had planned. Buck fever is real, as you have seconds to make a decision that could cost you a good shot or a poor one. I missed, and missed often, as they always came out the winner. I never got a deer with my bow in my first two years hunting, but what I did was start a love affair with family and friends about how much fun bowhunting was going to be in our lives.

Being in the woods was our sanctuary. Ed and I have been doing this long before our legal hunting age. We had BB guns at a young age, so we shot them until the barrels were about to melt down. It would be nothing to shoot one thousand shots a day. We learned how to be stealthy and then get as close as we could to the wildlife. As I said many times, we got so good with our guns that we could shoot bees off of flowers at twenty feet. Everybody still laughs at me and then tells me I'm full of shit, but we could do it.

Ed and I were walking down the road to a couple of fields that usually had deer in them. As we peered into the field, we saw three doe feeding about 150 yards away and decided to cut into the woods and try to sneak up on them. You have to watch where you step when trying to sneak up on a deer. Any snap of a twig puts them on high alert because this is their house. We managed to get within about fifty yards of those deer, but they knew something was wrong. They amazed me as we made no noise approaching those deer. They have a sixth sense that I feel no other animal possesses. The deer eventually got nervous enough to move on down the field and then scurry into the woods, heading back into their domain.

We returned to the road and then headed toward a trail that led to a hidden field surrounded by woods. Ed said there were always deer in this field, so we should be in for a treat. He wasn't wrong because there were about twenty deer scattered among the field. We belly crawled the next twenty feet to the edge of the field and then hid under some underbrush, gazing at some nice bucks. These deer had no idea that we were there. We lay there while watching these deer do their thing. It was starting to get dark, so I decided to make a *meow* sound so we didn't scare them away. Then to our surprise, the bucks started coming toward us. One came within about five yards, and then we started to giggle. The deer snorted and took off as the rest of the deer did the same. I looked at Ed, saying, "Why did they come to that sound?" He shrugged his shoulders, and then we got up and headed back to his house. Little did we know what we had discovered.

A deer hunting company makes a call that is a doe-in-heat call. It sounds a lot like the *meow* sound I made. It calls in bucks, as they think it's a doe in estrus, so they're ready to mate. These calls didn't come out till many years down the road. We were millionaires and didn't have a damn clue. We thought it was just some crazy cat sound that the deer came in to check out, as they are very curious animals that constantly walk on pins and needles. We didn't know what we had actually stumbled upon, but rich we did not become.

That night, we ate like any other dinnertime meal and then discussed what we had observed during our latest romp in the woods. We were quite excited, as archery season was only a short fourteen days away, and our scouting was a success. We were getting much more knowledgeable on deer patterns—what they ate, where they moved, and when they moved. We were much more skilled than the first year, where I just climbed a tree and then hoped a deer would get close enough for a shot. Things were looking up, but little did I realize about twelve hours from that moment, my life would be changed forever.

September 19, 1987

WE WOKE UP, ate breakfast, and then talked about today's game with Lakeview. We had a good football team with a lot of talent. I was a sophomore who started as an outside linebacker and a "killer" in the kickoff unit. A killer was a guy that just went for the ball carrier and had no gap assignments, just the runner. I loved kickoffs, as you just get to run full speed and then stick that return man. I got to them first many times. I just had the instinct to weave through the blockers and get to that return man. The harder you hit, the more it sets the tone for the defense, so killer was the right name for us.

We went to the school and then loaded the bus like we had done so many times before. I had no idea I wasn't going to be returning with the team in just a few short hours and then going to be in a fight for my life while just playing the fun game of football. I was talking about the great night I had with Ed, the girls we were dating, and the upcoming game about to be played. Getting hurt, being disabled, and needing help all my life at fifteen years old was never once on my mind. Breaking a bone, tearing a ligament, or just having a little injury is part of the game we play. You know this can happen in any play or any daily activity you do. You don't think about the risks; you live and then let the cards fall where they may. But nothing prepares you and your family for death or a debilitating injury. You don't think about it or see it coming. In a second, the life you lived before is gone. Let the game begin.

We were up 17–0 in the third quarter. There was light rain falling that day, but it was fun to play in those conditions. The kickoff team was going out on the field, and then the coach yelled to me, "Scott, get out of the game and let so in there."

I played a lot as a sophomore, but as I said, I love kickoffs. I yelled back, "Can't you find somebody else?"

He did, and then I lined up, ready to rock somebody's world. Only it was my world that was going to be rocked. I always think where I would be if I had just walked off the field. Sadly, you don't get that choice again. I've dreamed many nights about that short conversation with my coach, but the word "karma" has never shone

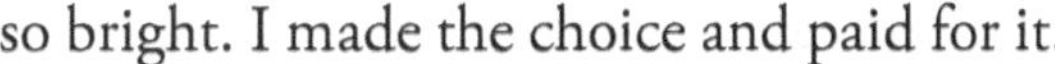

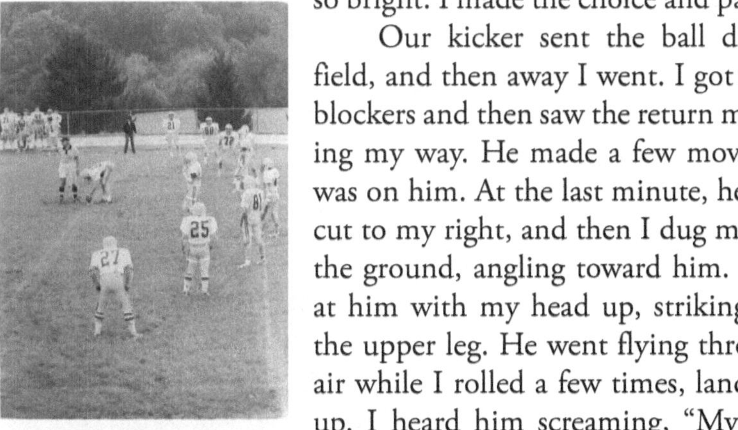

so bright. I made the choice and paid for it.

Our kicker sent the ball down the field, and then away I went. I got by a few blockers and then saw the return man coming my way. He made a few moves, but I was on him. At the last minute, he tried to cut to my right, and then I dug my foot in the ground, angling toward him. I lunged at him with my head up, striking him in the upper leg. He went flying through the air while I rolled a few times, landing face up. I heard him screaming, "My leg, my leg." I tried to turn my head and then look his way, but I could hear my neck grinding like a bag of rocks being rubbed together. Then my neck felt like a spring had sprung. I was like a jack in the box that you turned the handle, and then my neck popped out and bounced around. Right then, my buddy Jon grabbed my arm and tried to pull me up. I couldn't feel him do that, thinking it wasn't my arm, but I read my arm pad, and it said "Bidwell" on it.

I said, "Jon, don't touch me. I broke my neck." How did I know this? The Saturday before, I heard a college player tell his story about being paralyzed. He described the exact feelings I was going through. In that one or two seconds, I knew what had happened to me. Jon yelled to the coaches that I was hurt, and then they all came running out to where I lay. I said, "I can't feel anything or move."

The coach said, "You got a stinger. You'll be all right in a few minutes."

By that time, my parents both came out on the field. I could see on everyone's face that things were not good. My mom was crying, which just made things worse for me.

I yelled, "Get her the fuck out of here." I love her, but I just didn't need that shit at that point. I asked my coach how long it had been. He said about a half hour. I saw he was really nervous. I asked, "Does a stinger last this long?"

He said, "No."

I lay there, feeling the light rain hitting me in the face. They couldn't get a helicopter till the cloud cover broke up, but they didn't want to use an ambulance because of my condition and the distance. So I lay there for an hour with sprinkles on my face, hearing worried voices talking among themselves. I was very scared. (Picture above shows last seconds standing #27.)

The helicopter finally arrived in about an hour. I still had my uniform on and my helmet. They kept every-thing on me, moving me only when needed. As they put me in the chopper, I watched them put an IV in my arm. I didn't feel a thing, and then I started to cry. This is not supposed to happen to a fifteen-year-old kid in his prime. Like,  *What the fuck*, I thought. I won't be able to do anything normal ever again. Drive, date, hunt, fish, sports, work, and sex. What the hell am I going to do? I was in a very low place during that ride. Oh, did I say I hate flying? I was too scared to be scared during that flight.

SAINT VINCENTS

As they looked at the X-rays, they put me in a room with mirrors on the ceiling. All my clothes had been removed, and then I was as naked as a j-bird. I never felt them take anything off of my body. I was all alone in there, just staring at this lifeless body that, just hours earlier, was a tackling machine. I tried to move everything, staring at each body part for a twitch or some response from my brain. Nothing moved, nothing. I cried to myself softly as this was thrown upon me. I know nothing about what this kind of life will look like. I sure as hell hate it already. Maybe a miracle will happen, or something good…I didn't know anything. I was lost for the first time in my life.

The doctor came in, and they gave me the bad news. He said you broke the third, fourth, and fifth vertebrae. I would never move anything ever again. Was it a kick to the nuts? A very hard kick that I'd never feel again. He then talked about surgery and recovery. To me, it was like, who the fuck cares? This changes what, nothing. I'm going to be a cripple for life who sits in the corner, eats, pisses, and shits himself. An hour and a half ago, I had everything in front of me, but now I no longer cared if I was on this earth anymore. What do I have to even look forward to in life? To me, not much.

I had to have two surgeries. The first was to the front of my neck, and then the second was to the back of my neck. I woke up after the first surgery with a halo on and staples in the front of my neck. The halo was round and then ran about halfway down my head, attached by four pins screwed into my skull. Two in the front and then two pins in the back, with a brace around my chest with four poles that locked into the halo. Get ready for a six-month ride, folks, because it's not coming off for half a year.

A few days later, they basically did the same surgery, but now to the back. I woke up with a collar on but was happy as hell that the halo was gone. Not so fast, Scottie boy. In they came with the same setup. They asked if I wanted the pins in the same holes or new ones. I chose the same holes, and then they gave me a cloth to bite down on. I'm telling you, it hurt like hell every time they turned the wrench. Just turning into old scabs centimeter by centimeter. The pain was unbearable, but where was I going to move to get away? Nowhere. I couldn't move anything. I thought it couldn't get any worse, but it did. Next, I was placed in a Stryker frame. Did you ever in your life want to feel like a hamburger? I was the meat in the sandwich. They had a steel frame above me and below. Every two hours, they would flip me up, so I saw the ceiling, then down, so I saw the floor. Best part? They hung ninety pounds of weight off of my halo to pull my neck apart and then let the swelling in my neck go down. It felt like somebody was trying to rip my head off, having to endure this for about two weeks. During this time, I started getting movement in my shoulders and right arm. A few days later, the left arm started to move. All my pain had gone away in that very moment, as I thought it was all coming back, and I was fuckin' healed. Done, nope, that's all I got, but a lot better than the alternative.

During those two weeks, I had a morphine drip, giving me a limit on how much I could use. I'll tell you what, I was still screwed up. I remember a few moments that stuck out during that time. One, I had a girlfriend when I got hurt. She was crying when she came to see me, but I couldn't take it anymore. Like to my mom, when I was on the field, I said, "Fuck this, we are done." No emotion, no care, "See ya." Two, when Sanford and Son came on at seven thirty, no matter who was there to see me, I said, "Get the fuck out." It was my favorite show before I got hurt, and I guess after too. After a few days, people knew to stay the hell out during that show. Lastly, a teacher, who was also my football coach, would come up and see how I was doing. *Dutch* came just about every day. He would bring a *Playboy Magazine* with him on every visit. If I was flipped down, he would get on the floor and then flip the pages for me, and if I was up, he did the same. I remember him saying, "What do you think of that? Nice, huh." Those moments stuck out to me during that rough stretch of my spinal injury, but I don't remember a lot.

I got to think a lot during this downtime. I had a picture of Ed by my bedside of him getting his first buck. It was in the paper, highlighted by the words, "Dedicated to my friend, Beef." I got the nickname Beef from my dad when I was young. He called myself, brother and neighbor, Beef, Bacon, and Cheese. My name just stuck with everyone calling me that. Ed shot a ten-point buck that season, starting a streak that was almost unheard of. He has gotten a buck with his bow every year since. I cried as I looked at that picture because I thought I had lost one of the passions that I would pursue for the rest of my life. Never again would I hunt by myself or with my family. Tears ran down my face many nights while looking at that picture, with no way of wiping them off.

After I got out of the striker frame, they moved me out of the ICU and then to another room. They started exercising my arms more, and I could start to bend my arm at the elbow. But what I remembered the most was my gorgeous nurses. I thought I was the judge of a beauty contest. Many would come in after their hours were finished, listen to music, or read my many get-well cards. They put an extra pep in my step, even though I knew there would be no more steps. I was off the morphine, so my interest in girls was definitely greater than it was just two short weeks ago. But my question was, what the hell could I even do with one? Kiss her, then that's it? Don't sound too exciting to me. I was at St. Vincent Hospital for one month, and then it was time to go.

My family decided to send me to Harmarville Rehabilitation Center in Pittsburgh. As I was being transported down, the ambu-lance made a stop at my high school. The whole school came out and then gave me a wonderful send-off. I got to see a lot of people I haven't seen since my injury, and then they sent a shitload of balloons off. Before I could see many of my friends, we were off to my next destination.

/ / / / / / / / / / / / ▬▬▬

HARMARVILLE REHABILITATION CENTER

HARMARVILLE WAS MADE up of three departments: spinal cord, amputee, and head injury units. The place was fuckin' huge. It looked like a damn shopping mall. They wheeled me down the hall to the last unit in the place. It felt like forever. They put me in a room with a roommate, who was a cranky old man. While my parents were there, I didn't feel too bad, but when they left, it was very lonely. During the day, they took us to rehab classes, and then after that, they put us in the hall with the rest of the gimps or would set us up in the one room that had a big screen TV. You laid there all day just watching whatever the person who moved the best would want to watch. Dinnertime was the only exciting time you had as you could finally talk to someone. I know it wasn't hell, but it sure felt like it if you couldn't move. Things had to get better than they were.

After a few months, I started sitting up more and then tried pushing my chair around. I was getting stronger with exercise, feeding myself, and lifting weights. It took a few months, and then I started moving my chair farther and farther. The only thing that hampered me the most was my halo. You couldn't see shit. When they put it on, my

neck was angled up, and I couldn't see where to grab my wheels. I used prism glasses to see what was below me, but it was such a pain in the ass. I took showers on a flat grate. It was so damn nice to have water go through my hair and use actual shampoo. They did my hair and then my lower body only because they still couldn't get my halo vest wet, or it would smell like shit. One thing I did finally find out was I could get a hard-on. For the first time, I could see down with my glasses, watching my boy dance all around. That put a big smile on my face. The nurse said, "Little Beef, look at you." I used an external catheter. It was like a rubber, with a hole in the top that connected to a leg bag. They always stayed on better if they put it on when your pecker was hard. Hell, they have been doing this for months, but I could never see. It worked, so I was starting to smile a bit more. I learned though that he had a mind of his own, coming out when he wanted to. Better than nothing, as they say.

It was finally time to get the halo off. That thing came off so much easier than it went on. No pain just backed out the pins and then took off the vest. My neck was out of its grip, then moved so freely again. I had a blast just looking around from left to right on that ride back to Harmarville. I could wheel my chair without the use of those damn glasses and really see the world at a better angle. Things were looking up for this gimp until nighttime. As I was lying in bed, my neck started jumping, pulling from one side to the other. I was screaming for a nurse and then hit my call bell at the same time. My roommate was yelling at me to "shut the fuck up." I didn't know what was going on. The nurse came in and then asked me what was wrong, and then she left, coming back with deep heat cream. She rubbed it on and then told me that everyone went through this and that tomorrow would be a better day. It took about two days for the pain to go away. The more I moved my neck, the better it felt. Another obstacle conquered.

Once I got up, more things started to click for me, as I could now push everywhere in the whole rehab center. It still took me quite a long time to get from one end of the rehab to the other, but I defi-nitely got faster every day. We had classes that taught us how to get in and out of our chairs, stretch, roll, and then take weight shifts.

Others taught us how to write, feed ourselves, use adaptations, and, of course, sex. I sat up in my seat a little higher for the last one. I did have normal sex before my injury, but this sure didn't seem anywhere near as fun. I got the gist of it pretty fast, so I'd be on the bottom. Now I just needed to find somebody to fill that top position. Again, it was better than nothing, but I could live with that. I still use some of the adaptations they made so long ago. The first one fit on my wrist, having a hook on it. It was supposed to be used when pulling up my pants, but I use it as my finger to pull the trigger on my gun and bow. My fingers never worked after my injury, so this really was a great substitute for them. The second was a fishing pole holder. It was pretty slick, as I could cast and then reel with relative ease. Somebody just had to bait the hook. The giving didn't stop there, as Harmarville did provide other entertainment.

During these slow months of healing, I had a very worrisome visitor. Ed McConnell stopped by the rehab to see how I had been doing. Who is Ed? He was the Lakeview football player that I had tackled that dreadful day. I can't speak for him, but I'm sure he was very nervous and regretful. I made sure to put him at ease, telling him it was nothing but a freak accident. We talked about the play, shared sports stories, and then talked about our present lives. Things went well, I believe, starting up a distant friendship that began with us as just competitors. We have had conversations through the years, telling each other how our lives have turned out and staying friends till the end.

From time to time, Pittsburgh Penguin hockey players would stop by to talk with us. They made a deal that if you go swimming, they'd give us free tickets to their games. I hated swimming because I felt like a damn bobber, but I did it so I could go to the games. I did go to about five or so games and fell in love with the sport. The speed and physical style of play was right up my alley. What about that feeling you get when they score? Everybody stands (but me), and then the place just erupts into a frenzy, with the buzzer just screaming. I've been a fan ever since.

We also had many Steeler players come and say hi. I'm not a Steeler fan by any means, but the guys were very nice, taking time out of their day to come speak with us. The thing that stood out the most was their size. These guys were huge. The funny part was that they were defensive backs, or as NFL standards go, small guys. How big would the linemen and linebackers be? I was a good football player, so those smaller players would have been a handful to bring down. I think high school would have been my last stop in football.

I made a lot of friends down there in that unit. We all had the same problem, a damn spinal cord injury. We were all boys aged fifteen to twenty-one, and we all got hurt doing something with the risk involved. One was a star basketball player who dove into the ocean and then broke his neck. He had so high an injury that he couldn't move anything because I felt that same way many months before. You just can't feel sorry for yourself after being there because there is always somebody worse off than you are. Another was in a car wreck, but he had us baffled about his injury. From his shoulder to his wrist, he was paralyzed, but he could move his hand. We would laugh when we saw him holding his bad arm with his good hand when it had a pop or food in it. We would always ask him, "Can I have a 'hand' with this?" He would grab his bad hand and then say, "What do you need?" We were like a gang that would stick together until we all went our separate ways.

Others had almost all their movement in their bodies but pissed and moaned the most. I didn't hang around those "negative nellies" very much because they would just bring you down to their level. I guess everybody handles adversity in different ways, but when some of us were struggling to just feed ourselves, that shit got old quickly to me. You could tell the people who were athletes because we were very competitive, wanting to get better at the littlest things. Things most people didn't think twice about doing, we struggled daily trying to succeed in accomplishing them. I was getting a lot more posi- tive about what my life would be like because I never really thought about quitting anymore.

Mom would drive down every Tuesday and Thursday. It was good to see her, and I feel very grateful for showing up every week for the whole seven-month rehab session. We talked about what I was  doing every week and then what was going on at home. She always brought me some snacks and things I might enjoy. Dad would come down on the weekends, bringing Ed, Jeff, Carl, and my brother to visit on most weekends. Boy, it was good to see them. I love my mother, but I wasn't a mama's boy by any means. I needed to hear about hunting, fishing, and our sports teams—what was going on in the women's department and who was dating who. For my birthday, my neighbor got me a radio-controlled race car, and the rehab helped me set it up so I could drive it. Those guys also got one and then started racing them around outside. We made jumps and then little tracks to race on. It was so much fun that we took them inside and then raced them down the hall during bad weather. We got to be such a pain in the ass security shut us down. Those city slickers weren't used to "rednecks" coming to town and then running the show. My time at Harmarville was about to end.

By this time, I was the guy controlling the TV and wheeling 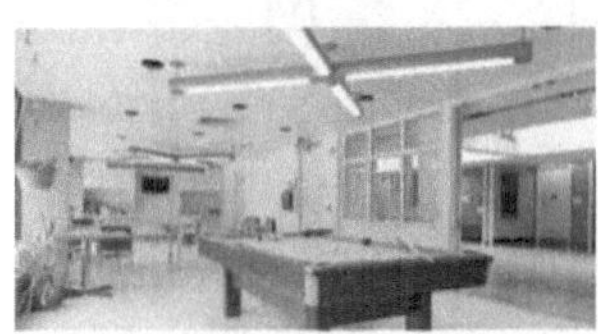 around the whole rehab, getting into trouble. My buddies and I would go upstairs to the vending machines and then get the good stuff. Order pizza and then have it delivered to the rehab center on many nights. The doctors would say, "Pizza was bad for the bowels," but it was damn good for our stomachs. We would go to the head injury unit and then watch whatever we wanted because those folks just stared out into the abyss. We had to be in bed by 10:00 p.m., breaking curfew nightly. Then you would hear them call our names over the intercom and then yell, "Get back to your unit!" We would still piss around for an hour or two. It was pretty much, "Get out," then my bags were finally packed, and to home I went.

BACK HOME

I MOVED BACK home, but to say it was a disappointment would be an understatement. I had such freedom at rehab because I could wheel my chair for hours and go anywhere in that mall-like atmosphere. I remember telling my mom, "This just isn't home anymore," and I could tell she felt bad about it, but it wasn't assessable as I was regulated to one room with a thick carpet and a bed. I know it wasn't anybody's fault, as that is what was there at that point of my journey. I had to get bed baths and then wheel outside to wash my hair. Everybody in the family helped out. When my parents worked, we got up early during the week and then were picked up by a school van. During the weekends, my brother and sister would wake me up. At that point, a thousand people saw me naked, so it didn't bother me too much, but it was a little weird having to put your dad, brother, and sister through that. Mom was a nurse and had me, so that was perfectly okay with me. My family having to put an external catheter on my pecker every morning did feel a little closer than I'd ever want a family member to get, but what were my choices, none? I'm sure they weren't fighting to get in line to do it either.

At this point, they were coming up with plans to build onto the house and then create a handicap-accessible part for me. It had a wheel in shower, an elevator, and a pretty good-sized room to maneuver my chair around. The community was absolutely the reason I got that new addition built. They had "Scott Bidwell" days across the region, raising over $90,000. That was incredible in those days because everything was word of mouth, by paper, or by news stations. No cell phones or GoFundMe like today. Students, families, and businesses all took time out of their day to help raise money for my room. I surely couldn't thank everybody for their effort and the kindness they displayed for a football player who just had a freak accident. I thank all of you still today. My addition was started during the winter months and was projected to be done by summer.

Once it was finished, I started to see my life as becoming a bit more normal and routine. They had a porch attached to the back of the house so I could go outside and sit in the sun during warmer months. I was like a damn snake, cold and sluggish, until the sun warmed me up. Just being outside was one of my favorite places, so some things never change, I guess. The elevator went to the basement, where there was a pool table and a big stereo system. It was the party spot and a place for all our friends to hang out. It was finally starting to feel like home.

To go out at that point, they had to lift me into our Suburban and then put my wheelchair in the back. It was harder, but we did what we could at that point to get around. My intent was to get out and then be with my friends, so off we went. That consisted of Jeff driving, Ed, Sean, Carl, my brother, my sister, and different girls riding with us every weekend. We would go to Meadville, then ride around the diamond to McDonald's, and back around the diamond for hours. It was fun, as you'd see friends who would get out of their cars, come get in ours, ride around another lap, and then run back to their group. It caused no harm, so everybody had a good time. They don't do that anymore and don't know if it was banned or kids just became too lame to do it anymore, but it's a shame, as it was fun. Oh, sitting your ass on the couch with a phone is more exciting, I guess, but I think it has ruined kids, in my opinion. That must be why their social skills and work ethic suck today. That's another story in itself.

We all started wanting the urge to get some beer but didn't know how. We heard through the grapevine that Petie in Saegertown would buy us beer. We approached him. He said yes, as long as we gave him "a couple of beers." We would get two cases of Budweiser pounders and then drive around the back roads or find some isolated place to park. Jeff didn't drink, so we always had a designated driver. The doctors said I couldn't drink on one of the pills I took, but I tried a couple of beers and amazingly survived! It was game on for me and my friends. We drank both cases every weekend, getting screwed up. Girls would get out to piss, and then we would turn the lights on. You could hear them yell, "You bastards!" We laughed and then continued to do it to them. I remember Missy puking out the back window as we were driving down the road. Ed and Debbie were always there, meeting up later in life, and got married. Sometimes, we would go to people's houses and just party there. It was such a good time, and then we all got home safely.

As we got a year older, Brian's house was our weekly hangout. Steve was seventeen, but he looked like he was twenty-five with his beard, so he was our new beer buyer. We would go there every weekend, getting tuned up each time. There was beer, whiskey, and smoke. I didn't smoke, as it was hard enough getting by my parents when my sister, brother, and I were so drunk. We listened to heavy metal music and then watched Steve do his best Ozzy Osborne's impersonation of "Crazy Train" on the drums every week. It was like a grand finale but very entertaining. He'd be pounding his drums and then ripping his shirt off at the same time. One time, Ed was gasping for a glass of water, so Sean reached into the fridge, giving him what he thought was water but grain alcohol. Ed threw up all over and yelled, "You asshole, that's not water!" Everybody was falling on the floor laughing, but Ed. Another Ed story. We were there for an afternoon party, with many people playing volleyball and sitting around drinking. Ed was sitting in a lawn chair by the edge of French Creek, which was right behind Brian's house. When Ed's hat was sideways, he was toasted. I saw him sitting sideways in that chair and then looked away to check out the game. When I looked back, he was gone. I looked around, didn't see him, and then asked, "Anybody see Ed?" Everybody said, "No." Then you could hear a faint voice asking for help. Everybody ran to the edge of the creek, and there was Ed hanging on to the bank, with his feet dangling in the water. Poor Ed. We laughed at him a lot. His mom is the sweetest lady, and his dad is a state cop who had me shaking in my boots a few times during my days there. He always said, "Boys, front and center," when we did stupid shit. His dad is so laid back now, but how Ed got past them after a night of drinking, I have no idea.

The next addition was a new handicap van that totally opened up my opportunities. The only thing I cared about was getting out and then partying. I could not drive my first van, so as my brother got older, he became my chauffeur. We headed up to Carl's uncle's camp to go trout fishing. There were about seven of us, and yes, we had beer. We decided we were going to go to the races at Smethport, so we all loaded the van and then headed east. We watched the races and then headed back to Kane. We found a bar there that had a rock band playing, so we stayed till closing time. We left and then found a bar still open a few blocks farther down the road. As we had a few beers, we met some people who said there was a party down the next road to the left and then said anybody could show up. So we loaded up again, heading to this party. As we drove down the road, we saw a place that had a bonfire with lights all over. We pulled in and then walked up to the party that had two tables, one with food all over it and then the other with booze. I don't know what everyone else did, but I stuck to beer, blacking out at some point. We woke up the next morning with the sun in our eyes and the sound of a four-wheeler revving up its motor. We looked around, noticing we were in a fuckin' cornfield. Jeff pulled down a side road and drove into a damn cornfield. I said, "Let's get the hell out of here. This guy isn't happy." To this day, nobody knows how we got there, but I live to talk about it.

The one that sticks out in my mind the most is the party we had at my folk's house. They were going away for the weekend, leaving around 7:00 p.m. They looked at all three of us, saying, "No parties."

"Of course not," we said.

Well, we told everyone to be there at seven fifteen and park at our neighbor's house, which was prearranged. While our parents were still there, we could see cars going down our neighbor's driveway and starting to park. They just went out the front door when people started coming in the back door. My grampa, Slick, as we called him, backed up the driveway, and then we helped unload a keg. We put the keg in ice and then put it in the elevator. Kids from all three local schools packed the place. We partied like rock stars. The next day, we cleaned up, smiled, and said, "We did it." A month went by, and then a friend of Brenda's told her mother about it and, of course, told my parents. Dad and Mom gathered us up and then told us we were grounded.

He asked, "What if somebody left and killed themselves?"

I said, "We kept all their keys."

Then he asked, "What if the police came?"

I said, "We put the beer in the elevator, and if they went downstairs, we would send it up, then upstairs, send it down."

He said, "Shut your goddamn mouth!"

I said, "Well, you asked."

Lastly, my mom asked, "Where did you get the beer?"

I said, "Your dad."

I know she shit herself and then thought it was a good plan, but we were still grounded. I thought it was well organized, well planned, and really fun.

I WENT BACK to school with one month left of the year but was tutored at rehab, so I stayed up with my class. I was like a celebrity those last thirty days, doing a lot of smiling. The best thing that happened to me was getting my grampa, Slick, to be my aid. He would push me from class to class, take notes for me, and empty my leg bag when it was full. I had two study halls at the beginning of the day, one for bullshiting and then the other for work. He would get so pissed at me and say, "C'mon, Scott, pay attention."

I said, "This class is for talking, and then next is for work." We would go in the back room, doing our work in the second study hall. One day, we were watching TV back there, and then we started flipping through the channels. We flipped to one, which was a little blurry but looked like a girl giving a guy a blow job. I got a little nervous, but Slick said, "Leave it there. We need some entertainment." Another time, he was pushing me down the hall, looking at a teacher's ass, saying, "What an assty day it is outside." He was always commenting on boobs and butts. I just sat back and then chuckled at his every comment. That must be why I'm the "ass man" I am today. I would take math tests, and then we'd argue about how I was wrong. Then after it was returned, I was correct. He would raise his hand and then ask the teacher how to do it. It might take the whole class period, but the teacher would take time to explain it to him. At times, he would fall asleep, knocking the book off the desk. The whole class would laugh. He would always yell at me for not waking him up, but even the teachers would say, "Let him rest." Slick helped make learning fun for kids and teachers. I was so lucky to have him involved in my life during this time. Everybody loved the guy.

I was shy at first with the women. Even with the sex classes we had, I still had to be alone, get undressed, talk her through it, and then dress me. When would my mom help out with that? Sure, honey, let me help you. Ya, right. So I just kind of blended in. I was an ass man, so one caught my eye one day at my sister's basketball game. I told Brenda about her, so we got in contact. We ate lunch together and then came to my house a few times. My family would move me out of my chair into a lazy boy, with her sitting on my lap. We would kiss and then talk dirty to each other, and it felt good. I broke up with her a while later because I got cold feet. She did nothing wrong. I liked her a lot but chickened out. I was never going to get any freedom or privacy at that point in my life, so I moved on.

My main focus at that point was attending sporting events with my friends. We had very good teams, so I followed them to every event. At that point, I was like the Panther mascot, and then I sat with my teammates near the bench and became another coach. Now the coach didn't listen to me much, but I had been with these guys since childhood, knowing their strengths and weaknesses. I knew where to put each kid to get maximum success, voicing my opinion many times, but mostly to deaf ears. Did it bother me watching them? Hell, yes, especially when things went wrong in my positions, as I knew I could have helped. Things stayed quiet for me through high school, so I just kind of went with the flow.

I do recall a funny event during my last prom. I picked a date earlier in the school year, and then by the time the prom came, we were just not getting along. I did go to the prom with her but then took her home after the prom, heading to a party afterward. We partied all night, deciding to stay there so nobody was out driving after they drank. I was put in a waterbed and then fell asleep for the night. After a while, I felt the bed moving up and down, but I couldn't understand what was going on. I looked to my right, where my buddy was banging his girlfriend on the bed beside me. I was thinking, *What the hell? I can't even have any freedom here, so there's not another place they could be doing this.* Well, the phrase "more motion on the ocean" is true because I felt that way. That would have been a perfect time for me to be away from home and get a little action, but I didn't have a girlfriend at that time. My time would come, and then I'd be ready. For now, I have graduated and am ready for my next stage in life.

Edinboro University

I graduated in 1990 and then got accepted to Edinboro University. It was twenty minutes from home, but one of the best handicap facilities in America. How convenient. They had power doors, a paved campus, and vans to take us to class. I really could push everywhere on that campus, having routes that could help me bypass hills and rough spots. Each dorm, school building, and office has a touch pad door. I'd fly down ramps, hitting the pad, then use my momentum to glide in the door. Now some doors were slower than others but would slam into them, getting jammed in them when it closed. I just had to wait for help, hoping it came quickly, or I sometimes freeze in the winter months. The whole campus was paved, so it made it easier for me to push around the campus. If there were hills, I'd go into a building, take the elevator up, and then be on level ground again. We could take the vans if we wanted to, but I pushed most of the time. I would use the vans in the winter because I didn't want to get stuck. A kid died one year when he wheeled home at night and then got stuck in a snow drift, freezing to death. I always had a buddy with me, so I didn't take chances like that while it snowed. Edinboro had a very nice system for us.

There were two dorms for disabled people. The boys were on the first floor of Shaffer Hall, and then the girls were on the first floor of Scranton Hall. We had a big concrete pad out front where we could sit and then collect the sun's rays. It was also the place where everyone went to smoke and relax. Shaffer Hall had four levels, so it went gimps, girls, boys, and girls again. As I saw it, that's more girls for us gimps, so I would meet out there and then have a smoke with some of Shaffer Hall's finest girls. I did meet a lot of girls on that pad, hooking up with a few later in the year. In the basement, they had a gym where we could lift weights and then work on our cardio. I tried to hit the gym daily for about an hour or so, keeping this quad physique in tip-top shape. About four of us actually used the room for working out, but others would come down to bullshit about their day. They also had a place where we could sign up for writers that we could use to help us take our tests or aid in homework. I learned real quick who the hotties were and then would use them during the afternoon to help me with homework. I met a lot of girls this way, dating quite a few. Lastly, they had personal care attendants on the first floor who did everything for us. They would help us in the bathroom, shower, get up, and put us back in bed. In this case, they were the closest people to us we had other than our parents. Some worked there for a living, while others were students. I became friends with many of them, dating a handful also. You would spend an hour to two hours with these people every day, talking about everything, with some of them getting very close to you. I said at the time, "Give me ten days with a girl. Then she would be mine." Did it work all the time? No, but I tried, most times succeeding. I was a lot better-looking than I am now, so I could melt them with my baby blues. I was starting to really like my independence.

I went to Edinboro, majoring in computer science. You spent countless hours working on programs with different software that I found very difficult for me. I continued to work with programs for two years, deciding I hated it. So I was a people person, wanting to have a career that involved my gift of gab. Since programming involved a lot of mathematics, I already had my computer credits and most of my math credits. I decided to become a teacher. Believe me, I was very nervous about my decision. How was I going to write on the board or grade papers? I had two years to come up with a solution.

When I went to a class for the first day, I'd locate some luscious babe and then go plant my ass right beside her. It was hard for me to keep up writing notes, so they gave us carbon paper. Girls have such beautiful handwriting, so reading their notes was a pleasure. During one class, I was beside this beautiful girl who was taking notes for me. Somebody forgot to clamp my leg bag tube, so piss was running out on the floor beneath me. I nudged her, and then she lifted up her backpack, and the urine continued toward the middle of the classroom. Every student in the line of fire was moving their shit. The professor lifted his glasses up, following the urine trail back to me.

"Mr. Bidwell, do we have a problem?"

I said, "No, you folks do," and then I wheeled out. Yes, I was embarrassed, as I had to wheel the whole way across the classroom, dropping piss streaks on the floor. But shit happens, right?

The next time in that class, the professor asked, "Everything good to go for today?"

I laughed and then replied, "I hope so."

I used to put my books on my lap so I could wheel around, not having to worry about holding one. A different girl was taking notes when my books fell off my lap and slammed to the ground. My legs were kicking, and my pecker was straight up in the air. That beautiful girl beside me grabbed those books and then slammed them back down on my boner. I couldn't feel it, but I felt like she knocked the wind out of me. She was just as red in the face as I was, with everyone staring at us. I felt like it was time to go and then wheeled out. I told ya, that thing has a mind of his own.

While at Edinboro, I learned that the professors hated hunting. They always scheduled a test on that first Monday of deer season, but I surely didn't want to miss such a tradition. I came up with the idea of putting red fruit juice in my leg bag and then going to the nurse's station. I'd complain of a headache, telling them I had a bladder infection. Anytime I really had one, I'd go to the hospital to get medication and sometimes be admitted. So I told them I would be admitted, missing a day of school. They wrote me an excuse for Monday, and believe it or not, it worked all four years. Those nurses don't want to dick with handicap bullshit, so they would gladly write a pass and then send me off on my merry way. I got to take my tests on Tuesday, with professors never knowing a thing.

After four years of schooling, I got a 2.85 GPA. Could I have done better? No doubt, but my mind was in twenty different directions. A healthy B was pretty good for all I had experienced, so I knew I could do better in the subject I chose to be my profession. I did my student teaching at Cambridge Springs High School first and then Maplewood High School second. I was familiar with both schools, so the teachers helped me with my craft. During that time, computer technology was in its infancy, so I used photo paper to make materials for the lessons I was going to teach. I'd call students up to write on the overhead projector to do examples and then do practice problems. I began to use the students at the board a lot more during my lessons, so it solved my writing problem and got students moving in the classroom. I could write well enough to grade papers and then mark them in their scores in the gradebook, having to hold my breath to write their grades in those tiny boxes. Then I learned how to make copies from the copier machine and then used them for homework and tests. When student teaching was finished, I received an A from both teachers.

September 19, 1987, is a day that will live forever in the memories of the Saegertown students and community. In a football game against Lakeview High School, sophomore Scott Bidwell ("Beef") received a serious neck injury when he tackled a Lakeview receiver and later was transported to Hamot Medical Center via Life Star Helicopter. Beef's spinal cord had not been severed, but had been traumatized; consequently, Beef had little feeling below his neck. The Saegertown community and students immediately commenced fundraisers to alleviate the burdens of the financial strain the Bidwell family faced. October 10, 1987, was declared Scott Bidwell Day in Meadville, with $10,300 being raised. Cards and signs filled Beef's room from well wishers; caring citizens called from across the nation to extend their sympathies and encouragement.

On October 28 Beef was transported to Hammerville Rehabilitation Center with the ambulance making a stop at Saegertown High School on its way. As the ambulance pulled into the parking lot, 500 students showed Scott just how much they missed him. While at Hammerville, Scott was not forgotten; Erie had a Scott Bidwell Day and friends continued to drive down to visit him. Scott came home for both Thanksgiving and Christmas and sent the students a letter he typed. Through the whole trauma, Scott has had a positive attitude and an undying perserverance to regain the use of his arms and legs. His strength and his zest for life are inspirations to us all.

We love you Scott!

PARTIES

I PARTIED A lot in my first two years. My number one hangout during those early years was College Park. You could wheel five minutes from the dorm and then pay three bucks for a red solo cup, letting you drink all night. We had to make sure we could get in and out okay because when everyone was blitzed, we didn't want dropped while leaving the place. I've been up and down some very big staircases. Scared going in, then not giving a rat's ass coming out, but I was never dropped during my drunken escapades involving stairs.

After a year of going to College Park, I went to DTOs Friday night happy hour. One of my best friends, Carl, was a brother there, so I always liked starting the night off early at five. I got to meet most of the brothers on Friday nights, parting week to week. Sean was a friend of mine who also went to Saegertown High School, playing on my many sports teams. We liked to party together on Friday nights, so we decided to pledge the DTO frat house. We had to do a lot of crazy shit. That entitled acting like we tied a string to our willies and then going around, asking girls for their signatures with a pen on the other end. We told the girls to be very careful because we did not want them to rip our buddies off. We also had to put dimes inside a bowl full of flour, with cooking oil on our faces. We then had to dig inside the bowl with our mouths, finding the dimes. Boy, did that make a mess. Another time, we had to drink Mad Dog 20/20 and then write down answers to questions that the guys asked us. From the beginning of the night to the end, we made an absolute mess on that paper. It was really something to see. During Greek week, we had to wear diapers with bonnets on our heads. On our hell night, we had to go back and forth across Edinboro on an absolutely drizzly, abysmal night. We would go to garbage cans and read where we had to go next, and then Sean would push me all the way across campus to the next clue. Then we would go all the way back across campus again and then get another clue till we finally got to the end. I got so cold. Sean dropped me off at a warm laundry mat, and then he completed the quest. Lastly, we went back to the fraternity, where they all gave us our jackets and then congratulated us because we were finally brothers. Jack was my big brother, while Jim was our pledge master. It was my first jacket since graduating high school, so it felt good wearing that thing. I still have it today at Mom and Dad's house.

In our dorms, we were not allowed to have beer at any point. I befriended the RAs, so I always allowed them to come down to have a beer in my room without any fuss. I was not twenty-one yet, so I had to find a couple of my friends to get me a beer when I needed it. If that didn't pan out, I would have my grandpa go get a couple of cases, and then he'd wrap them like presents and bring them to the dorm right in front of the RAs. I just chuckled under my breath because I thought it was quite hilarious. They had to have known. I mean, it was pretty obvious that both presents were exactly the same size and dimension. He always brought a case of Heineken or Busch Light for our festive nights. Anytime I was in a bind, he was the one who always came through. At least when Slick did it this time, we didn't get in trouble with my mom because she didn't seem to care that we were drinking at college. I don't know how close some of you are with your grandpa, but I will tell you what: that guy was #1 in my book.

I got my Social Security card when I was nineteen, so the date of my birthday was two years off, allowing me to enter bars at an early age. I'd show the bouncers my SS card, plus my student ID, and then they'd ask for a driver's license, but I would say I couldn't drive. That was all I had, working every time. Once you become a regular, they would never ask again. I liked the bars because they were a lot of fun, but they cost more. I used to be able to get into a party for three bucks, but now I spend twenty to twenty-five bucks. With a limited income, it was hard to go out to the bars and drink beer, so it was best to have beer at the dorm, where it was much cheaper per case. When you were in the bars, you met a lot of the people you've known since you were first in school, so you didn't get to see new people in those venues. You felt like Norm from *Cheers* when people walked by you. During the winter months, we'd have a school van take us to Pizza Hut, and then we would wheel to the bar. After a few hours, we have them pick us up at the hut. Bars were my least favorite because you were stuck in one place right by the door, so you really didn't get to the back of the bar to talk to anybody. During frat parties, I could wheel everywhere, which seemed to be my favorite.

Women of Edinboro

Now let's talk about the girls at college. My mom and dad dropped me off the first night and then helped set up my room so I was all ready to go. I didn't know anything about Edinboro, so I decided to head to College Park because that's what everybody talked about as the place to go. I saw guys going in a side door to a party and then asked, "Can I get in there?"

They replied, "Hell yes, come on, buddy. All you have to do is pay three bucks for a cup you can drink all night." So here I was, two hours from my parents leaving, and at my first college party. After about half an hour of drinking, a redhead came up to me, asking, "You're so beautiful. Could you lick my asshole?"

I didn't hesitate. I decided, why not go for it? This is what I've been waiting for ever since I was fifteen years old. I had my own place and privacy, and my mama was not going to be around for this one. So I sat her on my lap and then drove back to my dorm. I had a personal care attendant put me in bed. Everything started to escalate very quickly as she got undressed right in front of me. I did what she asked, circling the dirt track a few times, and then I had a little poo-tang for dessert. As a quadriplegic, when that dicky-do works, it works for hours. I did it! I felt like a man for the first time since tenth grade. At that point right now, I knew I could be with a woman. I'm so happy it happened that first day because it set me up for what was to come the rest of the time I was in college. And to be honest, I don't even know the girl's name and never met her again in all those four years at Edinboro.

The personal care attendants were with us 24-7. So, of course, I got to meet a lot of beautiful girls while they worked on our unit. One PC worked on the girl's side, so I would go over there for a couple of hours and then sit with her to talk while she was on her break. Some of the girls in chairs would be around asking if they could go out with me, with me saying no. I'm not going out with a gimp because we would look like two fish flopping on a bed. I'm not into that, as I want somebody that's in control. After a few weeks, that PC switched over to the boy's side and then would come in to kiss me while I was in the shower. We started to get pretty close to each other, spending all our free time together. Then one night, we went to the movies with a six-pack of cold ones, with my chair positioned at the very top back of the theater when a funny incident happened. I think the movie was *Twister*, where you could find her sitting on my lap as we necked during the movie. Well, I had to empty my leg bag, so I told her I had to go outside to empty it. She just opened the latch, letting the piss run down the middle of the aisle. I sure hope people didn't have popcorn in that aisle because if they did, it might have had a nasty taste to it. We went out for quite a long time, but she eventually had a guy who lived beside her that was hitting on her, so she left me for him. On a sidenote, I was going out with a different PC who worked that night when the old girlfriend ended up showing back up in my room dressed in a pumpkin costume with face paint. Well, after a while, I had paint on my face and all over my body, as my present girlfriend came in to find us together, sending me packing. It really wasn't even my fault, as she attacked me. Well, two girls were gone within a month. Let's move on.

Personal care attendants come and go, but one time, these two new PCs came from the second floor of our dorm. A buddy of mine and I talked to them quite a bit, asking them if they would like to go to a heart-shaped hot tub with us. She said, "You buy the room, we'll go." I was back in about fifteen minutes. The room is booked, so we were going up on Tuesday. I weighed about 158 pounds, with my buddy weighing in at about 205 pounds. They had a small front-wheel drive car that pulled in to pick us up. Since I was smaller, they picked me up, put me in the back seat, and then put my buddy in the front seat. We drove up there with the intention of getting buck naked with beautiful women. As we got there, they got him out of the front seat first and put him in his wheelchair. As they tried to move me, I hit my head on the back seat and then off the door of the car. Gave me a little bit of a stinger, but I was ready to rock because I knew it was ahead of us. We got to the room, where they gave us a bottle of wine, a couple of pornos, and some towels. As we went in, we noticed the mirror on the ceiling above the bed, a heart-shaped hot tub, and a VCR to watch the movies. They threw me in the tub first because I was in the smaller of the two. As I was sitting in there floating, they threw my buddy in there to my right. His dick was lying on my shoulder, then I yelled, "Would you get his dick off me?" The boy was hung like a horse, so it looked like I had a third arm. They moved his tower off me, and then the girls hopped in with us. We had a good time in the hot tub. They got us out, and then we lay on the bed, looking at each other in the mirror. We never really did anything except lay there, laugh, drink wine, and watch a few pornos. But it was a good time, only costing us about fifty-six bucks. I ended up going out with the one girl for about four weeks until she caught me in my room with my ex. Down the road I went.

I had a lot of one-time flings. As one girl was with me when I was on the toilet, she opened up her shirt and then stuck her boobs right in my face. She asked me, "What do you think of these?"

I replied, "I don't know. Let me find out." I had others who would get in the shower with me and then stripped down to nothing. They'd usually wash me, but this time, I washed her that night. One night, I was in bed at about eleven. A PC came in and then said, "I'll be back after work if you don't mind."

I replied, "Hell yes. Come on in. We can get to know each other." She was going out with a *gimp* on the other side but said that she went to a school near me. She said she always had a crush on me, even before college, and wanted to meet me. In my mind, this would be a perfect time to grant her wish. One night, I didn't go out because there was a blizzard outside, so a girl upstairs came down in a negligee, standing in my doorway. I've seen her before, talking a little bit, but I didn't expect what was gonna happen next. I shut the door, and then she undressed in front of me, helping me flop into bed. Then we got it on. Maybe I was terrible, as I never really got to see her again either. Another time, I was up on the third floor with three girls. I really liked that one as she was always smiling at me, and then she'd always stop to say hi. But I also had to include the other two to make her happy. We would play truth or dare, with me always choosing a dare. I said, "Take your shirts off and then do whatever you want to do." So they did. Then I was humming away on those boobies like I owned them. I thought about going a little further but decided that was enough for tonight. I was interested in one of them, so I didn't want to give any vibes to the others. I got so drunk one night that I ate corn on the cob and then threw up in the girl's hair while lying beside me. I thought she'd be furious, but she looked at me, asking, "Are you okay?"

I said, "Yes," and then she proceeded to go to the bathroom to wash the corn out of her hair. Can't say I'm too proud of myself sometimes. I'm so limited in what I can do, so if you like it or you don't, then I've got to move on to find somebody who does.

As I said earlier, a good way to find girls would be to sign them up to help write during my test. She would do homework with me and then show up during test days. I had her in my room one day, sitting on the floor, talking to me. I asked, "Do you want to do something that you'll remember for the rest of your life?"

She gave me a smile and then said, "What?"

I said, "Take off your pants, and then go set up on that desk."

I gave her a pillow to rest her head on and then went to work. My arms were pretty strong back then, so I could hold her in place for this midday thrill. She started whacking me in the head so hard that I started to get a headache. I backed out, wheeling back five feet. She fell off the desk and then started crawling across the floor on the bed, gasping for air. I wheeled over, touched her one more time, and then she screamed to me, "No more!" It seemed like we both enjoyed that nooner. I went out with her for quite a while, and that was a big deal because I never made it more than two weeks with a girlfriend while in high school. We would go to her house a lot and meet her mom, who was a cool single parent who did a great job raising her kids. We had a room adjacent to the kitchen, where her mom didn't care if we stayed together. I thought that was pretty cool because my mom would have had something to say for sure. While at my house, she had a one-piece on, and then she wanted to do things sensuously. She asked me to bite the crotch, unsnap it, and then I'd get a little present. I couldn't get that damn thing open, and then I bit her. She hit me so hard that I thought I had a concussion. It would have been much easier to just unsnap it herself. I think we were searching for things to enhance our relationship at that point. I know I'm limited, so we tried different avenues at every opportunity we could in the bedroom nightly.

One night after a party, she was grabbing ahold of my willy, stretching it like a Stretch Armstrong, trying to get my boy excited. It just wouldn't rise that night because I had a whiskey dick. She squeezed and pulled, but it just wouldn't do anything that night. You know, a mind of its own. The next morning when they tried putting an external catheter on, my pecker was so swollen the external wouldn't go on. My poor guy was black and blue. My best description of that moment was a hot dog in a croissant. You know, the kind you wrap the hot dogs in and then cook in the oven. That thing was so swollen up nothing would go on it, but it didn't take long for that baby to heal. That relationship ended one night when I was having a party in my room, and then someone came knocking at the door. I opened the door. The kid was rapping and then mimicking drumbeats. He drove me nuts. He asked if he could come in, and then I slammed the door in his face. She got up from her seat and walked out the door, ending our relationship. Yes, I was an asshole, totally deserving of it. I saw her kissing guys a few times at other fraternity houses. A few weeks later, she called me, saying that she made a mistake, but I had already moved on to another girl. We did see each other a few times years down the road, but nothing ever materialized from it.

My longest relationship came in my last year of college. Toward my final semester, I was with Dave at our favorite fishing hole. There was a girl who liked me, but I was just not attracted to her. She would ask me to attend parties every once in a while, but I would always tell her I didn't want to go. Well, she brought her roommate down our fishing hole. I looked at her, and then my eyes popped out of my head. She asked, "Do you want to come to a party at our house tonight?"

I replied, "Hell yeah, I'll be there."

There was a professor who seemed to be there with her roommate, and I sat with her. We got to talk about God, and I argued about points that he could not answer. Wow, he tried, but it didn't go well for him. When something bad happens to you, you ask yourself, "Where was God that day?" The professor and I argued most of the night and then went our separate ways. As we were leaving the place, her roommate came up to me and then asked, "Would you like to hang out some more?"

I said, "I'd like that too," and then we decided to call each other to find a place to secretly meet. We headed to a campfire along with a couple of my gimp friends from school. While we were drinking, she leaned down to pick up her beer, and I kissed her on the lips. She looked at me with excitement and then kissed me back. After the party, I drove her home, and then she sat on my lap, and we started to kiss. After a few minutes, she had her shirt off and did my best motorboat impression on those babies. This was the start of a fun but drunk relationship. Boy, that girl could drink for such a little thing. There wasn't a day that I could ever outdrink her, and I could drink a lot of beer. She was always two or three beers further than I ever could. She was over at my apartment one night. The apartment was so hot inside, and the air-conditioning was broken. It was pouring outside, so we went out to the balcony and then sat in the rain, drinking. It was right around that time that her roommate found out that she was with me. I don't think she was very happy, but hey, this girl was my type. I remember the first time I went to her house and then had to sleep down in the basement. They couldn't get me up the stairs, so I slept down there all night with a small heater blowing on my face, still seeing my breath. Now she was a late sleeper. I don't think she came to get me till 11:00 a.m. Boy, was I pissed. That happened throughout our whole relationship. She'd sleep in till eleven or twelve, and then I'd lay there waiting for her to get up. I was a morning person and could not stand getting up that late. I'd always hear her say, "Honeeeeyyy." She would drive my van back many times from her house, which is about two hours away. I'd lay on the back seat, and then she'd be up front with the cigarette, playing cheeseburger in paradise all the way home over and over. If I had an object-to-seat button, I would have sent her ass up in the air without a parachute. Unfortunately, I didn't have one of those in my van.

We were together all the time, either at my apartment or at hers. I had started student teaching around that time, and then I would always come pick her up after classes. She might have thought I was a knight in shining armor, but I didn't think I was anything that special. I did treat her well but kept a lot of fury inside me during those midmorning get-ups. During a sorority formal, we went to a holiday inn for the party. The party was in the basement, and there appeared to be no handicapped entrance. We asked around, and then an employee said we could go in by way of the kitchen. We weaved through a hallway and then through a new stainless-steel kitchen, heading through the door and finally on the correct level for the party. I just let her have fun with her sisters, drinking, dancing, and taking pictures. I didn't drink that night so I could drive everyone home.

After a few hours, everyone was ready to go, and we headed to the exits. Now remember, I had to go out through the kitchen to get in the place, so I headed back in that direction to exit the place. I got to the exit door, finding out it was locked. So I headed back down to the kitchen and then waited by the door while my girlfriend went to find an employee. I sat there patiently, and then my girlfriend pushed on the steel door, falling down onto my head and hip. We didn't realize that the door had the pins removed so they could move kitchen equipment in there. The door hit me so hard that it knocked me out, and then I proceeded to fall onto my wheelchair's joystick, spinning around in circles, squirting blood everywhere in that kitchen. My girlfriend tried to stop me and then eventually got me upright and started to come to my senses. I initially thought I was blind, as I could see nothing in my right eye. I looked around the room, and what was once shiny stainless steel now looked like a murder scene with blood everywhere.

I didn't want to ride in an ambulance and leave my van there, so my girlfriend drove me to the hospital, heading to the emergency room. I needed twenty-seven stitches on my head, and then I found out I had broken my hip too. Boy, do girls get me into trouble. She was so much fun, but everything eventually came to an end when she moved to her friend's house for the summer. I'd go to the races and then drive to her house, getting there late on many occasions.

One night, while coming home from Pittsburgh Motor Speedway, I stopped by, planning on spending the night. She had already had a head start drinking and was three sheets to the wind. Later, we went to her designated bedroom and then started to make out. She took off all her clothes and sat right on my chest. I was doing my duty, having a good time doing what I liked the most, and then I noticed that she was not getting excited. I looked down, and she had her head between my legs, with her back against my chest, and was passed out. Now I know there is no guy in this world that would ever complain about being in this position. But as a quadriplegic, I was finding out that I could not breathe. I tried to rock her from side to side and get her off my chest. I even tried to nibble on her, bite her, holler at her, or do anything to get her awake. At that point, I was getting nervous, as my air was running a little short. I started to holler, "Get off me! Get off me! God dammit! Get off me! Get off my fuckin' chest!" I always had the light on so I could see what was going on because, you know, I can't feel 90 percent of my body. In came the friend and her father to pick her up off my chest and then carry her to another room. They shut the door with the lights still on, no covers at all, just laying there buck naked. I stayed that way till the morning and then ate breakfast together, as nothing was ever said. We didn't seem to be getting along very well after that, but I did love the waterbed that they put me on that night. Her friend sold it to me, so my neighbor and I went down to pick it up, and then she showed up.

She then said, "Don't you come down here unless you call me ahead of time."

And I said, "Your fuckin' friend said we could pick it up now, and that's what we're going to do."

She didn't agree, and it was the first time I called a girl cunt. Now that word tends to really sting with women, and I felt some power in it. I liked her a lot. It really hurt me when we broke up. I don't think I really ever dated a girl again.

I know when I first got to college, I was terrified of being with a woman. The very first night gave me confidence that I used throughout my college years. I really wasn't scared of anything as I would approach any beautiful girl in the room. There were two choices: she would either say yes or no. If no, it didn't bother me, as I would just move on to something else. Something I also learned was the most beautiful girls in the place terrified most guys and made it hard for them to talk too. But I had no fear. I had the gift of gab and then put my baby blue eyes to theirs, helping us hit it off. I became more comfortable with my body and then fearless of taking it all off for the right reason. The only thing I had going against me at that point was I didn't want to be hurt again. There's nothing worse than being hurt by a woman. And yes, I did it to a lot of girls. I think back to my past and wish I could say sorry to a lot of the girls that I just went with for a few days and then sent them packing because of what they wore, said, or ate. I know a few years down the road, a former girlfriend said to me, "The problem with you is you're too damn picky."

I said I was sorry and then, in my head, I said, "Yes, I probably was."

I CAN'T END college without talking about the many mishaps I had there. And yes, many drew a lot of blood. One day, I was going to lunch with my girlfriend and all her beautiful roommates. I was showing off, flying down this hill approaching the road, when my front tires went in a pothole. My chair stopped abruptly, and then I flew out of my chair onto the road. Lunch was only scheduled for a few more minutes, so I decided to let them throw me back in my chair and go down to eat. I had blood on my head, my back, and my arms. But that didn't stop me from missing a meal, as I filled up with food as blood ran down my head.

Dave was one of my best friends up at college. We would always drink beer during NASCAR races, and then we would go to the bar a lot of times when the weather was better. One night, we were racing home from the bar, passing each other back and forth. One would take the lead, then the other. We got to the doors where you get inside our dorm, and then both went for the hole, slamming into the door and getting stuck. The Ras came and tried to pull us apart, but we were wedged so well that the doors wouldn't even close. They had to get maintenance to come down and then take the bolts out of the door so they could get us out. Well, RAs didn't look very happy that night as we argued about who won the race.

Another time, I was coming back from a party with a new girlfriend, approaching a hill that I didn't like going down myself. I thought she had a hold of me in the back, but as I was going down the hill, I started getting faster and faster. I turned my head and then saw she was still at the top of the hill, so I turned around to find a way to get out of this. At that point, the college curbs were not square but had sort of a ramp to them. I hit that thing, going about thirty miles an hour, and then I flew over the hill down into a swamp. As my girlfriend ran to get the cops, I propped my head on my shoulder to keep it above water. The cops helped right me as I thought I was going to get a DUI from being drunk in a wheelchair. Luckily, I knew them, and they let me off.

That same girl was pushing me another time when I was on the hill adjacent to the one I had flipped on before. Again, she let me go, and then I looked back to see her again at the top of the hill. Yeah, I was flying down the road again. This time, I hit the curbside and then slid along the concrete like I was sliding into the second base. I remember it scraped up my ear badly and the side of my face. I admit having a couple of beers in me made the pain much less intense. At that point, I stayed away from the hills with that young lady.

I was wheeling down the hill at Towers one day when my shoelaces got caught in my front wheels. As soon as it wound tight, I stopped abruptly and then flew out of the chair, slamming onto the concrete. I lay there for a little bit until some guys came and helped me up. Again, I had some scratches on me, but I survived again.

I was at a DTO party that got raided by the cops. Yes, I had my Social Security card, but I didn't want him to look into it and then have it taken away. So they lifted me out of the fraternity house and told me to wait right here. As soon as they went in to get another handicapped gentleman, I took off. I looked behind me, saw I was in the clear, then went to Pizza Hut, and hid in the bathroom until I felt it was safe. Then I left the restaurant, went around the backside of Edinboro, and went back to campus. That was a close one, as I might have lost my teaching certificate if I was busted.

The first time I went to spring break, I went with Sean and a personal care attendant. We didn't even have a room in Daytona, so we were going to be staying in my van. We stopped at Clemson University to see my buddy, Jeff. After meeting his roommates, Jeff introduced me to his girlfriend Terra, who became his wife a few years down the road. He took us to many parties and then to a dance club by the campus. I wanted to shake it up on the dance floor, so a football player from Clemson University just picked up my wheelchair and placed me on the floor. I found out from Jeff a year later he was drafted into the NFL by the Redskins. That boy was my guardian all night at that club. Jeff had a lot of influential friends at Clemson, many going on to the professional level. The next night, we got a twenty-eight-inch pizza delivered to his dorm and tried to put a dent in that baby. That was the biggest pizza I've ever seen at that point in my life. We couldn't eat it all. In high school, Jeff was our designated driver each weekend. He always had beautiful women with him, while I would usually get his scraps. I also came to South Carolina to attend Jeff and Terra's wedding. I got to see where he worked and then spent his free time with Terra. Jeff died after being stricken with COVID-19 a few years ago. He was always one of the strongest guys around and a great athlete. How could I still be alive, surviving after all I've been through? He was so strong and full of life. He did stop by the house a few times in the later years to visit. He was supposed to come up and see me a month before he died. He was such a good guy. I'll forever miss my friend.

After leaving Clemson, we went to Daytona. We didn't have a place to stay. Luckily, I met up with one of my buddies who lived in the dorms at Edinboro with me. It was just him and his girlfriend in a hotel room, so they invited us to stay with them. Sean and I would hit the bar scene in that Daytona area every night and then drink on the beach with the warm sun tanning our white Pennsylvania skins. Cars would parade by, with bikini-clad women jumping out to snag a beer from time to time. After a week in paradise, we made it home with no problems. The second year was definitely the trip of a lifetime.

Now on to one of my most interesting trips. Sean, Corry, Debbie, her boyfriend, Harry, and I were headed to spring break in Daytona for the second trip to Florida. Six of us were packed in my van, headed south, where the sun shone bright. We stayed in a hotel room that had two beds and a cot on the floor. I shared a bed with Corry. She would continually tell me, "No funny business." I had a girlfriend at that time who was also staying in Daytona, so Corry was safe this time. Harry was a fraternity brother who was also in a wheelchair and slept in the cot. Harry was in a drinking contest, putting down two pitchers himself. Well, that gave him the shits, so he used every towel and washcloth in the place and then had crap all over the bathroom. I don't really remember who cleaned it up, but it did get done. I remember drinking in my room with my girlfriend. Anytime I had to empty my leg bag, she just opened it up, letting it run down the balcony. Anybody who walked by probably thought it was raining, but there wasn't a cloud in the sky. At night, we just wheeled around Daytona, hitting the bar scene. There was always a party somewhere, but we always started with happy hour from 5:00 p.m. to 6:00 p.m. We would spend all our money on drinks, loading the table with alcohol, while booze was cheap. Then we could drink for hours, drinking everything we had lying on the table. We made out at that happy hour for the rest of the week. We had two days left in Daytona, but we saw there was going to be a northeaster coming up the east coast, so we decided to leave a day early to beat the storm. We got to the Virginia area, and then the snow got so deep that we could hardly drive on the highway anymore. We flew through the Virginia Tunnels while people were waving us down, yelling for us to slow down and not go. We came flying out the other side to continue our journey home. The snow got so deep we lost control of the car and then slid near the edge of a gorge, hitting the guardrail. We were screwed. A couple of our group pushed the van forward. We got rolling and then headed back through the tunnels and parked at the entrance. I know at one point, I called my mother because I was running out of pills, so she considered calling the National Guard to fly in medication for us. Well, that night, Sean and Corry were in the front seats while Harry and I were lying against the front seats. Debbie and her boyfriend were in the back of the van. We didn't have any food, so we ate the french fries that had been left on the floor from the day before. We melted snow on the car's heater so we could have drinking water.

The next day, they had enough of the road plowed, so we were directed to Bland, West Virginia High School. We were pretty much out of money at that point, but I did have my credit card, so I used it to buy three cases of beer. I remember sitting out in the truck drinking that night, watching guys grab beers out the school's window. Sean ran out in the knee-deep snow, then grabbed their case, and brought it back to the van. We now had four cases of beer. When those guys went to grab another beer, their case was gone, and man, were they pissed. I remember being in the auditorium, telling jokes and singing songs to the crowd. We were pretty hammered, so I don't really remember the response we got, but in my mind, we did a great job. We were fed bologna sandwiches when we arrived there, and I was quite pleased. Since we had two guys in wheelchairs, they allowed us in the bathroom first, and then everyone could get a shower too. The next morning, we loaded up and headed home. These folks were some of my best friends at the time, and I think we were totally sick of each other by the end of that trip. We still talk about that trip, still today.

I was at college at this time, but it was during spring break, so our family always headed down to Bristol Speedway for the NASCAR races. This year, however, I had a new weapon: a brand-new quickie wheelchair. This was a curb jumping chair that would go fast as hell. It was the fastest chair in the market at that time. We stayed at a campground that was across the creek from the speedway. In previous years, I had to be pushed around by my parents or girlfriend, which was no fun. This year, I could pretty much drive anywhere in the campground and race park. One night, I drank a few beers, and there wasn't much going on at camp, so I decided to check stuff out around the track and then see what was going on in the pits. To describe this track, it looked like an old mined-out hole, where the racetrack was settled inside. To get to the top, you had two asphalt paths that gradually went up a hill that was a football field length high. When at the top, the hill looked straight down. Well, I thought, *This is a good test. Let's get this girl up, baby.* There were no rails along the grades, so I went up the damn thing with no problem. I thought that was pretty cool, and then I proceeded to wheel around the top of the track, looking down in the pits and checking out the activity going on inside the track. I played around there for a while and then decided to start heading back. Well, the hill that I just came up about thirty minutes before was looking a hell of a lot bigger on the way down. Made it up. I'm sure I can make it down, right? We have clutches on our wheelchairs that stop us like brakes. But if it's too steep, they start clicking, letting you slide bit by bit. As I started going down the hill, my chair started turning toward the edge, clicking inch by inch. I was trying to make my chair go right, but it kept turning farther to the left. At that point, I was so close to the edge. I was trying to figure out a way to not move at all. I yelled as loud as I could, hoping somebody would hear me. Every time I did that, my chair would click another inch closer to the edge. I finally realized shit was going to hit the fan, so I tucked my chest down on my legs and then wrapped my arms around the frame of my wheelchair. I could hear my clutches start rapidly clicking, like a roller coaster, just before I headed over the first hill. Well, hold on, this shit is about ready to get real.

My front wheels slipped over the concrete, then into the grass, and down I went. I remember counting as I flipped down the hill twenty-five times. In my mind, I remember sky, ground, sky, ground, sky, ground. I just kept counting. A few times, I had a sky, ground, sky, ground, as I did a double flip before touching the ground. It quickly ended with the chair balancing on two wheels, then hitting the bottom, like sliding into second base. A lady and her kid came running over to me, asking how I was. She touched my leg and then asked if I could feel it. I said, "No."

She said, "Oh my god, you're paralyzed. Don't move."

I said, "Lady, I'm already paralyzed." Just then, her boy came over, asking me if I could do it again. I remember her slapping him and then telling him to go with his father. A few people came over later, finally propping me up. I could see that my armrests behind me were flush with the back of the chair. If my head would've been up, I would have probably ripped it right off my shoulders. I had little cuts on my knees and elbow and a slit on my head. I refused to get stitches, so they just put tape on it. Then I headed back to camp. And yes, I'll say that the new chair really takes a licking and keeps on ticking. I wheeled around the base of the hill, coming up the drive where my parents walked hand in hand. I saw my mom's mouth gasp open and then yelled, "You won't believe what I just did!"

My dad then asked, "You went down that hill, didn't you?" He continued, "Well, I wouldn't go down that damn thing in the toboggan."

I told them I was fine, living to tell the story. If I was smart, I would've owned half that racetrack because that was dangerous.

My years at Edinboro came to an end in 1994. I had finally graduated and then got a bachelor's degree in secondary education, teaching math. My mother asked me if I wanted to attend my graduation, but I didn't care to go at all. I'd been there, done that. I knew just about everybody on campus, and I didn't have to see one thousand people get their diplomas. All I cared about was mine, so I stayed home. At that point, I was totally sick of school. I've done all the partying and studying one can handle in four years. I was now comfortable with women, had a degree in math, and was ready to move on with my life. Boy, was that a fun time. Everyone should have a chance to experience such a ride.

APARTMENT LIFE

I HAD BEEN in Edinboro for four years but wasn't ready to leave just yet. I got an apartment with my buddy Dave and two other girls. The first night there, I was staying all by myself, so my dad asked me if I'd be okay, and I said yes as he left. I had some PCs lined up to take care of me, so my nighttime guy put me to bed. At that point in my life, I had a lot of spasms in my legs, so they would kick uncontrollably at times. While in bed, they started kicking, then my body shifted toward the side of the bed. I couldn't do anything about the kicking, so I slid onto the floor. I was like, "Shit, what am I going to do now?" Well, I laid there till my morning PC showed up laughing. I was relieved that I wasn't alone and still stuck helplessly on the floor. The morning PC was gayer than a two-dollar bill, always calling me "beautiful." I let him know I wasn't interested the first day I met him. He was very flamboyant and very comfortable in his skin about being gay. He would always ask me how I liked those dirty old poo-tangs, and then I'd shoot back with "And you like to stick yours where?" He was fun in the morning, always telling me his male escapades. I was like, "Okay, had enough there, buddy." We all laughed at him and with him.

While I was there, I took a few classes at Edinboro to work toward my master's equivalency. I was a lot more serious about school and doing much better in my classes. Now that didn't mean we didn't party, as every night, we would scratch together six bucks to get another case of beer. We would drink old German pounders every night. The cases cost ten bucks, but if you had all the bottles and then returned the case, you'd get $4 toward the next case. Every night, we would have different friends show up, some showcasing their skills with a guitar or harmonica. My night PC played guitar very well, coming up with cool riffs each night. I started putting words to his music, and then we started playing the songs every night. After a few weeks, we had seventeen songs and then would go play at frat parties and bars. We made two copies of our songs, but both were lost at some point during our travels. I believe my PC took one and then my girlfriend at the time had the other. I still know some of the words and recall each song's beat, but those tapes have never been found. Our songs were about life and experiences we have had. I've always said that the heavy metal bands I've listened to have the best lyrics and sound when they were on drugs or drinking. We always had our old German on hand while creating a song or musical note. We just didn't have the same creativity if we were sober. It was definitely something I had always wanted to do, so I did it.

When it came to food, we were on a very tight budget. I would always get a loaf of bread, then a couple of pounds of bologna and cheese. I'd also buy the cheap mac and cheese, five for a dollar, to keep our cupboards stocked up, so that was always on hand. Dave would have his deer meat available to the rest of us, with the girls always having ramen noodles available, but I hated them. Stupid noodles. I thought they tasted terrible. When we had extra money, we ordered a lot of pizza from John Wildwoods. That was the best pizza joint in the town, as they would deliver till four in the morning, which we had to do a couple of times. I always liked my wings from Hunters Inn. They didn't have many places up there that tasted as good as them, so we didn't eat a lot of wings. Best thing about pizza is it can feed a lot of people at a reasonable price. You'd get two pieces each, and then everybody would practically kill each other if we had a piece or two left. If there's anything you could say about this, our diet was not very good.

There was always somebody at the place, but one night, it was just me and my girlfriend. My bed was folded out in the living room, so we didn't really want to stay in that room because everyone outside could watch us. So I went to Dave's bed, where he had a comfortable egg crate mattress, and we could move his bed into any position. Of course, my girl took off my external, and then we played around a little bit, having a good old time together. She forgot to put another one on, and then I pissed in Dave's bed, getting his egg crate all soaking wet. It smelled like a county home, so he wasn't very happy. I remember seeing that thing hanging outside on the balcony, trying to dry out. We cleaned it up and then washed it the best we could, but it was never the same. Sorry, Dave. I can still hear him today, "You sumbitch." I laughed and then said, "At least you got a piece in your bed, buddy." Dave passed away at home a few years later after an infection in his blood. He was my twin. So lucky I got to meet him.

Since I finally graduated from school, OVR was in the process of getting a van I could drive. After my driver's test at the Edinboro parking lot, I was ready to drive myself. On my eighth practice day, my instructor asked me to drive to Corry, and then I felt like I was about ready to shit myself. Up till this time, I was just practicing in Edinboro's parking lot, where there was nobody coming the other way. He said, "You can do this. There shouldn't be any problems." I drove all the way to Corry and then went to the state police barracks. A policeman sat in the car with me, taking me around to different areas to test my driving. I was nervous as hell, so I didn't even want to look left or right at that point. I whipped that van right into a parking spot and then asked how I did. He said I passed with flying colors. I drove the van all the way back to the college and then unloaded with a great smile on my face. I finally crossed off one of my biggest challenges and, to date, an achievement I'd never thought would be obtainable in my situation.

I FINALLY GOT my first van, which was a green Ford. I no longer had to wheel around campus, as I could just drive to wherever I wanted. At that point in life, gas was pretty darn cheap, so I had no problem just getting in my truck to go for any distanced ride when I used to wheel around. It was about this time that I applied to a bunch of schools about subbing. I was in Penncrest School District, Conneaut School District, and Meadville Area School District. I had worked just about every day, but I liked Penncrest the best because I was familiar with that school and a lot of its teachers. I went to Conneaut a few times, but it was so far out of the way, so I didn't really know anybody. In Meadville School District, I really liked Cochranton, as it was a laid-back small school that I really felt comfortable in. Now Meadville High School has a different story. The first day I subbed there, I had two kids shouting at each other in the back of the room. They were saying fuck this, fuck that, then yelled at each other constantly. I sent them both to the office, and then a few minutes later, they were sent right back to me, saying that that's not a reason to send them to the office. I shrugged my shoulders, seeing how things worked there, deciding not to sub there if I had any choice. I did like the vo-tech though. It was interesting, as the kids were really in-depth about what they were doing. It was a lot of hands-on activities, which I strived at when younger. I remember one teacher in my local school telling me, "Do your job like it's your own. You couldn't just go there, sit with your feet up, and then let the kids have a study hall if you wanted to get a job." I took that to heart, always doing my best every time I subbed. Then I got myself into something entirely different than I envisioned.

DURING MY PARTIES at DTOs, I met a guy named Greg. He owned a pizza and Sub shop over in College Park. I always enjoyed the Subs because they were monstrous and the best in town. We talked about a pizza shop and then decided to go in together, starting one in my hometown. It was one of three pizza shops in town. We did very well, but the only problem was I couldn't take over a spot because Greg had to run his own pizza shop in Cambridge Springs. Yes, I could be there, but actually making the product, I could not do. I was subbing every day and then trying to run a pizza shop later in the day. In my mind, I felt like it was a little too much for me at this point. Any employee we got was usually at a younger age or a high school kid working for the first time. I had good supervisors for morning and night, but many new kids could never be up to speed on a busy Friday night. After a few years, we would see money start to come up missing at night. Since Greg couldn't be there and I couldn't be there all the time, I didn't see a reason to keep the place open if I couldn't run it correctly. So I closed it after four years of operation. I really wished I could have been more knowledgeable about how to run a business because I was very green in that area.

While working at the pizza shop, I got a call from Penncrest School District asking about an interview for a full-time job. It was pretty intimidating sitting in front of all those school officials. I remember the one question they asked me, "Should everybody learn algebra?"

I replied, "Heck no. There are people who make the rockets that go to the moon, there are people who pay for the rockets that go to the moon, and there are people who wonder what the hell is going up there to the moon. You're never going to change the way that is because everyone isn't as skilled in math. Students shine in different ways. They usually have a talent in one area or another, so let some grow elsewhere. That, of course, doesn't mean skipping your math courses, just that a good variety builds the résumé."

The next day at the pizza shop, I received a call from the superintendent, asking me if I wanted to be a Panther. I said, "Hell yes." At that point, I was a full-time teacher and a pizza shop owner, and I haven't told you yet, but I owned a race car on the side too.

TEACHING JOB

WHEN I DID student teaching, I taught about two of the five days per week. Getting kids for five straight days every week was very tough on me at first. My plans were not very good, so I had the kids at the board more than anything else, and they were not writing the lessons in their notebooks. They were not retaining the material. After the principal's suggestion, I decided to make notes that they could write on the board and on the paper to keep in their notebooks. This seemed to get the ball rolling, as I probably got my best PSA scores for the seventh-grade kids. The year before, they were not as good, and I took that to heart and decided to really put forth a better plan together to raise their grades. It felt good to finally connect with those kids, and that resulted in more advanced learning. I loved seventh grade, as they would jump through hoops for you to make you happy. Throughout the years, our school got more advanced in technology, and we started to use computers more often than overhead projectors. I was very reluctant to change at first because things seemed to be working with me. I decided, at one point, it was getting tough to make copies for my classes, and just entering grades in a book took forever. First, we got big screen monitors in the front of our classrooms and then computerized grade books. Both of them were a godsend, as now I could spend more time on my lessons and prep time. When COVID-19 came, I was prepared for the homeschooling transition. Kids were home for weeks, but I still had to do lessons each day with them. Thank God for the aid of a computer, or I really don't know how kids would have gotten lessons daily. During regular class hours, students would log on with their iPads and then join your class. We would have to take attendance and then check homework just like before. We had outlines that the students could click on and then get that day's lesson in an instance where they missed class. Lastly, you could produce tests that were graded with the click of a button and then register them into the gradebook. Why did I wait so long to incorporate this? Like most people, I hated change, so I thought it would create more work. I did learn my lesson, drastically enhancing my teaching. We could talk at any point during this time, so it was pretty easy for me to get the point across to a kid who had a question the parents couldn't answer at home. It did have some drawbacks though, as it was hard to sense their individual personality. Students worldwide lost that constant connection between teacher and student. The two years of COVID hurt education immensely.

As a math teacher at Saegertown, I was the low man on the totem pole. I didn't get the highest level math students, as most of my kids didn't enroll in any classes beyond algebra 1. But you know, I loved those kids and could associate with them. I was never poor or had parents who were divorced, but many grew up in a difficult family atmosphere. I taught them that math wasn't the most important thing in their lives, just a bump in the road of life. I was more concerned about them living every day to its fullest and don't be afraid to try something new. I knew these kids weren't all going to be good math students but could be very talented in some other interest that you're going to do every single day. So those kids would really give their best effort during my class, and I was very happy when they mostly improved. I know some teachers think if a student is failing in the classroom, they will fail in life, but some students have great work ethics and talent in other areas outside of school. One thing I stressed on the first day of every year was when you get out in the real world, nobody gives a crap about you until you show them what you can offer. I said, "Get a taste of all the food and then find a dish you like most." Many of my students went on to very successful careers and did not attend college. Kids will find their way. Sometimes, they just need a little nudge.

Now on to the good, the bad, and the ugly of teaching.

The good—it kept me young, and I could feed off the energy it gave me every day. I loved their personalities and anyone who could give it back to me when I joked with them. When students started off slow, then a light bulb went off, and they thrived. When I could fly through a lesson in one day, and all the students gave me a look of understanding. A student showing interest in my hobbies and daily activities. I did a lot with students in my personal life because they might not have those opportunities in their home or that parental figure that they didn't have in their life. They would help me when I'd take them fishing, hunting, or to the races. Some went on to find a trade or pursue a job that paralleled what I loved. Teachers always say, "If I could only get to one kid, I'd do my job." I got too many of them.

The bad—the kids that just gave up and threw their whole life away. I was good at reaching kids, but some just never gave themselves a chance. They didn't want to try anything, and sadly, I knew where their future was heading. When you hate the world, it's hard to let somebody in to help you. I'll tell you that I really tried to get some of those kids to open up and let me in, but they refused to let me in their space. Those kids would miss forty to fifty days a year and never try to get caught or ask for assignments. I'm sure it was their homelife or lack thereof. People go through rough patches, but you are on this planet one time, and you must claw your way out and try to better yourself every day. Putting yourself behind the eight ball before your life even starts is why these kids struggle in life. Such a shame really.

The ugly—yeah, I had a couple of these kids in a downright brawl. One time, two girls in my study hall were arguing over a boy, and I sent one to the office. She was walking out of the room, and the other girl grabbed her and started pulling her hair and kicking her. The one kicked the other in the crouch, and she went down, moaning like she was dying. I tried to get between them, as other students aided me in getting them apart, sending one to the office and holding the other one until everything calmed down. We had to move one of them to another room to solve that ordeal. Those darn boys.

I had kids throw chairs in my room that bounced off my desk and the walls. You thought there was a riot going on in my room. They were fighting over a girl, and the testosterone was flowing. I had about twenty boys in that class, with no females present. I know both of these guys, and they're good friends today. It was always something about girls or boys that drove kids into WWE fights. I kind of know the feeling, as I would puff up like a chicken when a rival sniffed around my girl too.

Then you'd have the ones that would say, "Fuck you," while walking out of class.

I'd say, "What did you say?"

He said, "Fuck you."

And I'd say, "I didn't hear you."

"Fuck you," he repeated and slammed the door.

So I'd write them up for three "fuck yous." Then they wouldn't be in my class for a while, and it's just good to get rid of that negative vibe because students do so much better without distractions. I never had a fear of getting involved in a confrontation because of the physical sports I played, and I didn't mind getting in the middle of this stuff. It sure was nice having some of the kids get involved because they knew I might need a little help. Kids were always helpful, from doing class activities to helping restrain somebody. It doesn't sound right, but it was true.

What was my teaching style? Yes, I taught math, which was the most important part. As a teacher, I believe you should be the entertainer that puts asses in the seats. I went through a lot at their age, so to pass that on to them, let kids know anything could be possible for them. I said, "You are so far ahead of where I was at fifteen, so go achieve your goals." Some of their problems were basic, while others were more enduring, but I tried to give them hope that anybody can overcome their adversity through positive thinking and will to succeed. Kids would come to me after class and describe their problems, and I would do what I could to give them my best answer. I'm not a father, but I see 120 kids a day in my classroom, and I see what makes them happy and sad and when they need an ear to talk to. Then I always tell them about some of my crashes and embarrassing moments. It really puts them at ease, and their problems aren't really that big of a deal. Most of my kids are not going to college, so I told them, "You guys can make just as much money as any of those college grads. Go to vo-tech, get a trade, and do something you like to do with your hands and mind." They are all good-paying jobs right now. The biggest thing was don't ever give up, as there's always a better day out there.

And as I wrote this book, I told you how I felt as I went along and didn't think there was anything left for me. One of the things kids liked was listening to music during tests. Music always eased my tensions and loosened me from strenuous activities. The only problem was that I had to listen to my favorite heavy metal music, but I used slow songs during the test. I had a student text me the other day and tell me he listens to nothing but the music I played him in class, so I know it was sinking in. I also did this when we were doing our homework. As I said, it lets people tap their feet, relax, and think about fewer things while doing math. And actually, the math gets better when you're at ease. We laughed a lot, and to me, that's what it was all about.

The teachers. Yeah, I don't think my personality fit in with some of them, but I think I got along with just about everyone. I never took charge during meetings, as I would just sit listening to suggestions, duties, and information about kids. Basically, I would just shut up and do my job. I was very close with about three teachers in my school and spent most of my free time bullshitting with them. I would stop in for a talk or two with most of them, and I also loved my aides. Most were in my class to help the learning support children, but they would help me with daily activities too. Just writing on the board and answering questions really helped keep the class flowing. We were all striving for the same outcome: the development of a child's mind.

Teachers all had to eat, so during lunch, we had our best laughs. We had a divider where most of the women sat up front, and the guys sat in the back. Now some of the women chose to eat with us, and they would piss with us just like we would with them. I remember one funny story that sprung up one day. Somebody started talking about the average penis length of a man and said it to be 5.75 inches. Then one of the females asked, "How long's that?"

I said, "Somebody give me a dollar bill." I said, "Well, that's six inches right there."

She said, "Well, that's not very long."

I said, "Wow, girl, somebody give me another dollar bill." Boy, did we all laugh. It was a fun group that allowed you to be yourself and say your peace without constant ridicule. Another time, a certain female would get on the microphone and start giving announcements. One of the teachers would get up on a chair by the speakers and act like he was giving it a knob job and kept saying, "Na, na, na, na." If you had food in your mouth, it was coming out. God did we laugh, and I had to wipe tears from my face. If you were stressing before you came in, you sure as hell weren't when you left, as it was the finest time-out a teacher could take midday.

We talked a lot about sports and what was being played at that time of the year. We would have brackets for the NCAA tournament and distribute them to the faculty. I never won and had shitty luck most of the time. A faculty member who picked her favorite colors of teams won it one year, so go figure. We did fantasy football leagues where you would have thought we were all general managers and getting severely underpaid. Most of the guys didn't hunt, but I talked about my adventures every season. I got my buddy Rick interested, and he's been hunting with me for about seven years now. I told him how much fun it was, so he bought a bow and came down to join camp with us. That poor boy hasn't gotten buck yet, but boy, he sure has been close.

I had a few funny episodes in school and at that point in my handicap career, but I didn't get embarrassed anymore. I had just finished lunch and was in my room teaching statistics. I was on an antibiotic for a bladder infection, and my stomach started making crazy noises. I felt my face get warm, and then I heard that dreadful sound of crap popping in my pants. I sat there for a second, wondering what to do. I took a sniff, hoping that it didn't move on to other people. But it sure did. The whole class started looking around, wondering who dealt one. My cousin was an aide there, so I went down to her room quickly and said, "Hey, can you go to the office and tell them I need a sub?" I waited in the classroom till another teacher relieved me, and he walked in and said, "Oh my god!"

I just put my chair in high gear, saying, "See ya," and wheeled out the door toward the office. I didn't like the principal or the vice principal at that time, so I made sure I went into their office, sat there, and told him I was going home. I wanted to let that linger just a little bit, and then I headed to my van. I drove home and had a personal care attendant waiting for me. She started to get me out of my chair and noticed crap went out the back of my pants and then down over the wheels. It was in my tires and all over the floor. I decided to call the school and let the principal know she might want to check the hallways as I think my chair spread shit all over.

She replied back, "I know."

Nothing like a good crap in the middle class. The next day, the class discussed my eventful day and had a good laugh. Humor eases all pain. On to the second story.

I was teaching in class one day, just wheeling around the room and doing my thing, thinking everything was going to be great today. At the end of the class, a girl approached me to ask, "Mr. Bidwell, do you wear underwear?"

I thought for a second about how I was going to answer this and why. I said, "No, I do not wear underwear. I just put pants on because undies just get in the way."

She said, "Well, you should because your nuts are hanging out."

I looked down and had a tear in my pants, as there were my boys hanging out on my lap. I said, "Thank you very much."

She asked, "If that happened to me, would you tell me, as I don't want to be caught with a tear in my pants either?"

I laughed, saying, "Sure I will, and I'll do it after class like you did." What girl would do that? And to keep a straight face? Not many, I think. I put a book on my lap, covered my jewels, and then went ahead with my day. Got to love how some kids respond to adversity.

I also had a mishap in life during that time. I like to party and drink a few beers here and there. But this one set me back a few bucks. I was at my sister's wedding, partying like a rock star. At about one thirty in the morning, we decided to pack up and head home. I felt good to go, having no fear of driving drunk. I had my grandma with me, holding cupcakes on her lap in the front seat. While going home, I wanted to take a back road, but they were under construction for bridge work, so I headed the long way home, going by the county home. There was a sharp curve by the county home that I took to the inside to cut off the corner. Unknowing, a cop was sitting there, watching my move, pulling me over, and then asking if I'd been drinking. I said yes, I was at a wedding and had a couple of beers. I actually had more than a few beers, but by the time I'd quit, I had a few hours to let them wear off. I took a Breathalyzer test, and there was nothing registering on the unit. My grandma was yelling, "He has low lung capacity." They decided I needed to go to the hospital to get a blood test to see what my blood alcohol was. They didn't want to put me in the cop car because they were worried about hitting my head and hurting me, so they called in an ambulance. I took the ambulance to the hospital so they could draw my blood, figuring out it was a .13. A .10 level was legal at that time, so I was now considered a DUI driver. It felt horrible, and I was very embarrassed about it. The first thing I worried about was telling my superintendent that I had been caught driving drunk. I went to him and then told my story while he sat there looking at me. He said, "Son, I've been on both sides of the road myself but was never caught. It happens, but don't let it happen again, or you'll not be a teacher here at this school."

I said, "Thank you. I won't let you down." From that day on, I never touched another beer except when I shot my buck. Lesson learned. So glad I never hurt anybody. The worst thing at that point? That ambulance ride cost me nine hundred bucks. That sucks. Plus, my dad had to drive me to school for two months, dropping me off for work, which was so embarrassing. Never again.

I know they told us at first that we should not be friends with the kids, but some turned into my best buddies. As you know, I like hunting and racing, needing help in both to make things work. My dad and some of my local buddies were always the guys that would help get me in the woods and do the things I needed to create a successful hunt. As everyone grew older, they kind of did their own thing or started a family. They would still come over at times to help me out. But if you know me, I'm dedicated to whatever I'm doing and never missed a day in six weeks of hunting. I would be out when it's nice, rainy, during winter, and even during thunderstorms or tornado warnings. So as my dad got older, it was getting a little tougher on him to keep up with me. I started using kids that were in my class or interested. I'd take them from school to the woods and then back to their home. If you know the kids, then you start knowing the families too. Everyone starts to take part in one way or another. And like my friends before, as these kids got older, I brought new kids in to help me out and do what they love also. I probably witnessed six of my students shooting deer while I sat in the blind with them. I love shooting buck myself, but nothing is better than being in the blind as a family member or friend gets to harvest a deer. You just create a memory that the two of you will never forget. Most days, they just set me up and I hunted by myself, and they would hunt from a stand many yards away. So basically, I was really not alone. They hunted and then came to get me out after dark. We own the property, and they would be allowed to hunt there if they were helping me out.

HUNTING

WHEN I FIRST got hurt, we were not allowed to use crossbows in Pennsylvania. The only time I could hunt was in gun season. After a few years, people with a disability could hunt with a crossbow in Pennsylvania, and I must tell you, the bows at that time did not shoot very well. It might be on for three arrows and then shoot two feet to the right with the next arrow. Another thing we didn't have at that time was a blind that you could set up in the woods. Dad had a four-wheeler made for me. I sat on the back of an old wheelchair that was cut out and mounted to the back of the four-wheeler. It was hard to get close to a deer when you had a four-wheeler, a man, and a kid in a wheelchair mounted on the back, sitting in the woods. Deer are hard to get close to, and they sure as hell didn't want to get close to us, but we did have our chances. The damn bows weren't very good in the early years. I missed a mounter one time at twenty feet. I put it right on his chest, and it shot right between his legs. It sure felt like getting punched in the gut when I saw that thing run off.

My dad asked, "What the hell were you aiming at?"

I said, "I put it right on him, and I saw the arrow fly between his legs." Oh, what a shame. One night at Marshes, we found a hot spot. There was a hot doe getting chased by about six bucks. My dad was turning me from left to right. We couldn't get on the damn deer at all. We'd get ready for one, and then it would run off, and then another one would come in. What we did find is one hell of a good spot for bucks. It was hard for Dad to lift me up on the back of that four-wheeler, so I decided I wanted to hunt out of my chair.

For about $2.85, I went to the hardware store to make a bracket that could hold my bow that was mounted to my wheelchair, and that's when I started hunting off the ground. The deer would always see me because we didn't have the use of blinds yet. I'd always try to tuck behind a tree or some brush. Those darn deer always pick me out. I did shoot a little buck my first year of archery season, but it got a lot better once blinds came out.

That next year, I met a student named Jake. He was in my class and also interested in hunting. I used to post the kid's pictures in the back of the room when they shot a deer and could tell who was interested as they would share stories afterward about their hunt. Jake and I became friends. He then started setting me up in my blind and hunting on our property. We had a lot of luck, and we always had nice bucks around us. Since I could now hunt out of a blind, we got to see a lot more deer that were much closer also. I wasn't lucky enough to shoot a big buck every year, but I did harvest a buck every archery season. For me to harvest a buck, the deer had to walk right in front of my blind. It couldn't go to the left or the right, but it had to walk right in front of me. Do you know how many nice bucks I had to see walk right by me and I couldn't do anything? If I tried to turn my chair, it would make a noise, and the deer would run away. So I had to sit there quietly, hoping one would step in front of me and give me a shot. But like I said, I hunted every damn day, hoping a buck would make a stupid choice, and walked in front of me. That hot spot produced a dead buck for twenty-three of my twenty-six years hunting. I shot two other bucks at the gas well and only had one year where I didn't harvest a buck. Here are some of my favorite stories.

We had purchased a six-wheeler to equip so I could go hunting. I rode in a few times and then had a gun rest mounted on it so I could shoot. Hunting season was supposed to start the next week, so we had everything prepared for that first morning. While I was coming home from therapy that week, I could see a cloud of smoke billowing into the air close to my house.

As the van drove closer, I could see the smoke was very close to our house. Finally, pulling into our driveway, I could see our garage had totally engulfed in flames. My brother jumped into the six-wheeler and tried to start it up, but apparently, it had a gas leak. When he hit the ignition, it blew up and sent him up into the rafters. Luckily, he got out, but the whole garage burned to the ground, including my six-wheeler. We had a week till hunting season, and there was no vehicle to aid me in hunting. Then we came up with a plan to take an old wheelchair, cut the bottom of it out so it's just the seat and a leg rest remained, and then mount it to the back of our four-wheeler. You could turn it on a plate that would swivel about 120 degrees each way. Then we slid a gun resting on top that would hold my gun and shoot any direction about 240 degrees. My dad pushed me toward the direction of the deer, and all I had to do was pull the trigger. It worked like a charm. Thanks, Big Rich.

My buddy Carl took me hunting one day about a quarter mile down in the Blooming Valley swamp. It was snowing very hard that night, but we still decided it was a great night to hunt. Toward dark, Carl rattled in a nice buck. You can rattle deer horns, and then bucks come in to check out who's fighting. We did get the buck to come in close, but it busted us and ran up the hill. After dark, Carl tried to start the four-wheeler, but it wouldn't start. We played around with it a little, then realized the fuel gauge wasn't turned on. We hit the switch, the four-wheeler started up, and we took off toward the hill. Carl drove through a creek, hit a rut, and I heard a loud popping sound. Just then, my chair fell off the back of the four-wheeler, and I started rolling down the hill. Carl thought he killed me and ran down to prop me up. He leaned me against a tree and said he was going to go get help. Carl got on the four-wheeler and started going up the hill. After a minute or so, I could hear that the four-wheeler had gotten stuck, and Carl started yelling, "What the fuck! What the fuck!" Carl ran back to say the four-wheeler was stuck and needed to run up the hill to get help. As I lay there, propped against a tree, all I could think about was that Carl was a smoker. He's probably going to die of a heart attack running up that hill, and I'd be stuck down here forever. Carl finally got out of the woods and told the property owner that I needed help. They called my mother, but my dad was hunting in New York, so she didn't know who to call. She called Butch's Pub, and a bunch of the patrons came to the woods to help get me out. After about an hour, I heard a tractor coming down over the hill with a toboggan dragging closely behind. They sat my chair up on top of the toboggan and dragged me up over that hill. There were like ten guys who showed up to help get me out of there, nine from the bar. Thank you, Butch's Pub, Carl, and Mother, for that one.

We bought land and then built a hunting camp in 2001. Seven of our family members put money into the camp, purchasing 147 acres of land. Dad always said we had to own our land if we wanted to hunt anymore because everybody was posting their property. The first year I hunted in gun season, I would stay at camp. That lasted only one night. I'll tell you why. I woke up in the morning with my dad getting me out of the bed, which was located on the first floor of our camp. Well, as he took the covers off, my pecker was sticking straight up in the air. Guys were eating breakfast around the table, and then one of them yelled, "Would you put that thing away? I'm trying to eat." I was so embarrassed. I never spent the night at camp again. I would always just get up early at home and then come over before daylight. That solved that problem.

I also had an incident that happened in camp after a day in the cold. After a long day of hunting, I was sitting in front of the heater, taking a nap. While sleeping, I was awoken by a watery substance running down my face. I looked at my fingers when one of them had melted down to the knuckle, and then my fingernail dripped onto the floor like it was in hot wax. My first thought was "Oh shit, Mom's gonna be pissed." Three of my fingers got third-degree burns that day, but one of them never really healed correctly. We tried to let it heal on its own, but the skin never grew back over the bone. I remember taking the bandage off in classes because the kids wanted to see what it looked like. If you've never smelled dead flesh before, I did. It is terrible. I would bend my finger at the knuckle, and then you could see all the bones and tendons at the time. Well, I got the news I was expecting that I had to get my finger amputated. The surgeon cut through right at the first knuckle, flayed my skin like a fish, and then sewed it back on above the knuckle. I asked him if I could keep the bone, get it chrome dipped, and then put on a necklace, but he wouldn't give me the finger because of the chili law. People would put body parts in food and then try to get money for them. So he threw my finger right in the garbage as I wheeled away. I now have four and a half fingers on my right hand.

Like I said, I've killed twenty-five bucks in twenty-six years of hunting, but my best memories were of somebody else sitting in my blind spot and killing a deer. Jake hunted with me once and grunted at a buck for about a half hour before he finally gave us a shot. He came to the left side of our blind, and Jake pulled his bow back. His arrow was three inches from my face. I had to lean back so he could get a shot. He smoked that deer. We were high-fiving and happy as hell. It took a while to find that deer because it didn't bleed that much, but we found it very close to the blind. Jake made a great shot on that buck. Another time, Jake and I were hunting for a doe. I'd already gotten my buck, so Jake was sitting with me to help out. Guess what steps out? A nice buck. I told Jake to take the bow off my rest and shoot because he had not yet harvested a buck. He slowly took the bow off and took aim. He dropped that thing right in his tracks. It was a nice seven-point that had me more excited than any of the bucks I've ever harvested.

I had Jake's girlfriend Cassie in my blind once, and she shot her first doe. She was a doe-killing machine but could never get a buck anytime I was hunting with her. We did see a lot of bucks, but they never gave her a shot. I remember Cassie made me a plaque for school that said, "Thanks for taking me hunting. It is very memorable to me." It was covered in Turkey feathers, really standing out in my room. Cassie also set me up on a date one day. I know this isn't exactly a hunting story, but I was hunting a friend of Cassie's. I always thought Miss Tri-City Speedway was a very nice-looking girl who always talked to me and was a lot of fun. I went on a date with her to the Rustic Inn in Hydetown, and Cassie accompanied us. I ordered wings and then chatted with the girls until our food came. When I bit into my first wing, I felt my pants erupt as I started shitting myself. I was very worried about that girl smelling me, but I lucked out and had an air-conditioning unit right behind me. It would suck up all my shitty stink into the air-conditioning and, thankfully, send it harmlessly outside. I finished my wings, paid my bill, and got ready to head out the door. I made sure that the girls walked in front of me, held the door, and then quickly zoomed through the door. I hoped neither girl smelled me, said goodbye, and headed out to the van. I got in my vehicle and started laughing.

Cassie asked, "What's wrong with you?"

I said, "I shit myself and just wanted to get the hell out of there."

We drove home with the windows down the whole way and just laughed. We know how to make a date exciting. Thanks, Cassie.

The next student to come into my classroom who loved hunting was Cassie's brother, Trav. Trav also became one of my best friends and had many great hunting memories. One of them pissed me off though. It was the first day of archery season, and we were heading down to the blind in the dark. With a flashlight, we could see a buck looking at us, standing ten feet in front of the blind. We got in the blind, waited till light, and heard a heavy-footed deer run away after it smelled  us. Soon after, a small six point that was there in the morning came walking out and stopped right in front of us.

I whispered, "I'm not shooting that deer, Trav."

He said, "Come on, buddy, it'll be a hell of a memory, you and me together, bringing down that buck."

We went back and forth arguing about shooting this deer, as I really didn't want to shoot this buck and end my season so quickly. After Trav chirped in my ear repeatedly, I pulled the trigger and dropped that buck. A couple of guys pulled into camp afterward and saw the deer hanging there.

Trav said, "Come look at Scott's buck."

I yelled, "Don't even look at it! Trav fucked me on the first damn day of archery!"

He just laughed and then said, "That was a great memory, bud."

I felt like he ruined my whole year, but it was ultimately my decision, and I regretted it big-time. To this day, he always brings that hunt up as his greatest memory.

Another time, I was with Trav early in his hunting career, and we were trying to shoot a big doe. After pulling his bow back, I observed where his arrow was pointed, and it looked like Trav was going to hit the ground way in front of the deer. The lift on his arrow rest never came up, and the arrow hit the ground and bounced between the doe's legs ten yards away. He missed that deer by a mile, and then it ran off. I was like, "Where the fuck were you aiming?" We looked at his bow and saw that the rest was loose. Soon, a little doe came out, and it was my turn to talk him into shooting a deer he didn't want to.

He whispered, "I don't want to shoot that little thing."

I said, "Come on, man. We're buddies. This would be a great memory."

Well, he shot it, and we still talk about it today. Trav still hunts with me today. We put cameras out to see what bucks are on the property before the season starts. He always tells me, "I'm gonna hold out for a big bastard." That never fuckin' happens. He usually shoots big bucks within the first week, but he just hasn't gotten that real big daddy he has been looking for. He is definitely a deer killer and one of my best friends.

Then there was Lonnie. He wasn't the best student, but that boy had a work ethic that most would fail in comparison. He was by my side for every racing and hunting event. The both of us were crammed into my blind every night, and he helped me harvest two of my bucks. He didn't have a hunting license at the time, but he loved to be in the outdoors, hunting during every season. After buying his license, I gave him the chance to shoot one. He used my bow and then waited for an opportunity to shoot his own white-tailed buck. We were sitting in a blind, and a nice buck was walking  along the woods toward our blind. It turned and then started walking away from us. Lonnie turned the bow to my right, barely scraping my chin, attempting to get a shot. Lonnie was a big boy, so the scope hit the top of the blind window, and he couldn't see the deer. I was like, "Lonnie, you gotta kneel down or stand up to get a shot." He stood up, and then the blind lifted off the ground eight inches. It had to be a sight to see for that buck in his last moments of life. You could see my wheelchair tires and Lonnie's boots below the bottom of the blind. He made a hell of a shot, and then the buck expired sixty feet from the blind. I felt bad for the guy because we were the only guys at camp that weekend. The rest of our hunting crew went to New York for their hunting season. One time, my buddy Rick shot a nice buck. He made a good shot on it and then backed out, waiting for help. Nobody was at camp yet, so Lonnie volunteered to help Rick find him.

I said, "Lonnie, do not chase that deer. If it's wounded, just let it die, and we'll find it later."

He went with Rick, snuck up on the deer, and said, "I'm going to go run it down and jump on its back."

Rick then replied, "Lonnie, I don't think that is such a good idea."

Lonnie took off after the buck. It then ran off toward the swamp, and we never found it. That was a bad move on Lonnie's part because that deer would have died and probably did. Poor Rick still didn't have a buck yet.

I had already got my buck one year, so I was going to go out with my dad. His bow could only shoot about forty yards, so he grabbed my bow because it would shoot fifty yards or farther with no problem. We started walking up the trail behind camp, with my chair making a ton of noise.

Dad said, "We're not going to see a goddamn thing with all the noise you're making."

So I decided to drop behind him about thirty yards and then move as quietly as possible through the woods. The bucks were running at this time of the year because they were in full heat. You might see a big one anytime you're in the woods, so you have to keep your eyes open and your ears on full alert. I was watching my dad take one slow step at a time and then saw his ass cheeks clench and grow tighter together. I knew then that he had seen something big. Big Rich pulled the bow up slowly, took aim, and then shot. I saw a huge buck run down through the woods as we were debating whether or not he had hit the deer. After hours of looking, we could not find his arrow or a drop of blood. He missed that deer. We think the main culprit was a rosebush that was located right in front of the deer before he shot. It deflected the arrow and then sent it down through the woods, hopelessly disappearing into the woods. He didn't get that buck, but it was a fun memory to have, all because of those tight ass cheeks.

Since we are talking about Rick, he was my fellow schoolteacher who heard all my hunting stories and then wanted to try hunting himself. He bought a bow and then came to camp to practice till he was shooting a nice group of arrows. He did have a few nice bucks come in one time or another, and Lonnie kind of screwed up finding the one buck he hit very well, but my buddy never did score on a white-tailed buck. One time, we were hunting when this little doe walked in beside us. It looked like the bucks had been putting it to her all damn day. Her hair was all fluffed up, and her coat appeared to be dripping with sweat. She took a few steps and then lay down beside us to take a nap. We were just laughing in that blind for about half an hour. That poor doe looked like the corner whore, but we never saw her daddy. Rick and I also had a funny memory that was not involving hunting but racing. Rick had a yellow jeep that he took down to Butler to run off-road courses with other jeeps. He said he was entering the jeep parade, where jeeps around the area would come down to Butler, compete against each other, and then head down the road in a parade. At the same time, my brother and I left work and then headed down to Lernerville Speedway to pick a pill for the upcoming racing event. We drove ahead of the race car so we could pick a pill and then filled out the registration at the track. As soon as we got off Interstate 79, heading toward Butler, the parade had started. We followed jeep after jeep at about fifteen miles per hour, arriving at the track too late to pick a pill. We had to start dead last on the field and then didn't make the pill draw through racing. I blame everything on Rick because he had to have his buddies in that damn jeep parade. Every time I see a jeep now, I just shake my head and then think of Big Boy. Damn you, Rick.

One day after work, I called Josh. I asked him if he wanted to hunt my blind, but he was already in his tree stand and didn't know whether he wanted to sit with me. Everybody knows my blind is a hot spot, and there are always bucks walking by. He called back and said, "I'll meet you down at camp, and we'll head to your blind." I really wanted to be out that night because it was drizzly and cold, and I knew bucks would be moving during those conditions. We sat there most of the night, not seeing any deer. Then right at dusk, I saw two bodies coming down along the edge of the field. The first one walked out and stepped right into our shooting lane near the apple tree. Then the second one came in, jabbing the small six point in the side, and started eating apples where the smaller buck had previously been. It was a huge buck that stood broadside thirty yards away. I started to tell Josh to take his time, but I didn't even get that out of my mouth when he shot. He double lunged that big boy, and it ran over to our left about fifty feet and fell over. I remember the excitement in his voice when he called his dad to tell him he shot a monster buck. They were all asking how big it was. Josh wouldn't even let me go over to see it or drag it out before his dad got there to show him. Boy, that deer was a big buck. You should have seen the smile on that kid's face. That totally made my damn day.

I also took my sister's kids hunting. Peytyn was a hell of a hunter because she would sit quietly, look all around, and never make any noise. It didn't matter if it was too cold or hot; she never complained. One morning, we were hunting in my blind, and a spike came in about 8:00 a.m. I had seen this deer daily com-ing in at about the same time every morning. It came down the trail like clockwork and then turned right before Peytyn could get a shot. I was so pissed off.

I was swearing under my breath because I thought that we had screwed up our chance of shooting a buck. About a half hour later, a nice buck came down the same trail, but this time right in front of our apple tree. She did not miss that buck, leaving me giddy inside. I was so proud of her because she handled the whole situation like a pro.

Now Ryder. He was a bumbling mess in the blind. He was always on his phone, rustling his feet in the leaves and kicking the blind constantly. It really drove me fuckin' crazy. I under-stood that he was young, but I kept taking him out. We finally had that little doe that Rick and I had seen come walking down the trail beside us. Ryder was about ready to shoot that doe when I saw a buck walking behind him. I told him to wait a second because a buck was coming behind it. That buck walked right to the apple tree, and then I told Ryder to put his forty-yard pin on him. He shot, the buck jumped, and then took off running. He went a little way, but Ryder did end up getting that buck. The smile on his face keeps me interested in this sport, passing it on to the next young kid so he can have the chance to hunt like I did.

This was a crazy day one time when I was hunting with Matt Latta. We saw nineteen doe that day, ending a great morning in the woods, and we couldn't wait to get back to camp to tell our story. I was backing out of Marsh's driveway, getting very close to hitting some trees, when Matt told me to turn around and then go up the other way, so I did. When I started going up the hill, the bracket that held my chair down let go, flipping my chair back with my hand on the accelerator. My van took off, ramped the road, and then hit the ditch on the other side. I had a Velcro strap across my lap that had let go, sending my ass to the edge of my seat, and blood came out of my lip from hitting the steering wheel. I looked over at Matt, and he had blood coming from his face after he hit the windshield. Just then, my buddy Jake was coming down the road and saw the whole accident. He came to my window and then asked if everyone was all right.

I said, "Yes, but how's my truck?"

He said, "Well, your rear tire is about six feet off the ground."

I thought about what he said for a second and then found out whether or not this van was bent or not. They pulled me out and then started driving down the road. I could only go ten miles an hour, or I'd lose control of it. The frame of my van was bent severely, so I lost my van for about six months. That really sucked because that was during hunting season. I blame that all on Matt.

As you read the stories above, yes, we got deer most of the time. That was our goal: put time in the woods, outfox the smartest animal, and hoist that buck up on the meat pole. But it was the laughs and time together that meant more to  me than shooting any deer. I know there are people out there who harvest a big buck and then don't tell anybody about it. Why? The stories are what keep the hunting camp alive. It's not easy to get a big buck. Some guys hunt for years before even shooting their first buck. I like what my dad always told me, "It's called hunting because if it was easy, it'd be called getting, then everybody would be doing it." They call me the general at camp because I just do not let the guys give up. I have to motivate the troops and get them out in the woods, even if they're tired and had a miserable day hunting. You can't get a deer sitting on the damn porch. Another famous Rich Bidwell quote. Dad taught me a lot about hunting, and I passed that on to many of my friends during our great outdoor adventures. It was a lot of fun. Thank you.

RACING

NOT ONLY DID I have hunting buddies, but I also had racing buddies. I had about six or seven kids from my high school that would have helped me. I also had three or four students from other high schools who would help me. During downtime, you got to talk to these kids and you found out their interest. So after school, we would head to a racetrack or garage. I would pay their way into the races and purchase their food, and in return, they would help me out with the car. Not only after school but on the weekends as well, it would be nothing for them to be there two or three days working on that thing until late into the night. Racing is a second job, or you're not doing it right. I wore the white hat but couldn't really do anything in the car, and I would aid them and help them walk their way through problems. There's no better education than getting your hands on something. That's the way I was when I was young, as I would tear everything apart to find out how it worked and then put it back together. When I broke my neck, that was something I really lost, but now I had to use my mind. I got to do that while working on these cars because I knew what was wrong with things, but I couldn't really do it myself. These guys would always listen to what I said and do what my hands used to do. I raced for twenty-four years, so as kids got older, I moved on to find other race enthusiasts. I can thank Joe, Tom, Jake, Jake, Cassie, Justin, Theo, Cody, Mike, and Lonnie for all the great years together. They all put in countless hours and time from their lives to help me live my dream. I got to see all these ladies and gentlemen grow from kids to young adults. I never saw them complain about two- to six-hour drives or late nights in the garage. Their weekends were busy from morning till getting home between twelve and three in the morning. They learned what heartache was and how great it was for everything to go your way sometimes. Most important, the only person that gets a fuckin' trophy is the guy that wins. You got to earn it, not have it handed to you. What a lesson. Hard work rewards you.

I had two other guys with whom I spent most of my racing career turning wrenches, and it was our mothers who brought us together. When I first met Tim and Matt Latta, they were twelve and fifteen years of age. Throughout all my years of racing, I raced with the Lattas most. They were kind of into hot rods until I came along, as they could take what they learned from Grampa Marv and use it in racing. It was basically being able to turn wrenches and put a model together. You got pieces and parts, plus a pile of bolts that go here and there. Yes, there is a lot more to it than that, but knowing that gets you started. These guys were with me through just about everything, from building the car, setting it up, tuning the motor, and putting the decals on it. That is it, folks. Not too hard, right? Here's how it all began.

When I was two years old, my dad would take me to the races, and I'd sit along bleachers and make a dirt track to race my little cars on. I was only about four feet from the wall and just got accustomed to that sound, as dust was flying through my hair and got dirt in my diaper. We were always involved with some kind of racing, but dirt was our style. Dad used to take us to all the local tracks, and we would go from Friday to Sunday every weekend. That was our home where I felt the most comfortable as if I were one of the gang members. My dad's friends got involved with a couple of race teams, and sometimes, they had their cars in the driveway at my neighbor's house. I'd always be over there drooling over those cars as if they were God's gift to me. Now we had a car to follow, so we headed to a racetrack every single weekend. We would pack our family and dad's friends into our Suburban and head over to Ohio every Friday and Saturday night. Sometimes, we would go racing three times a week.

I was a very skilled drawer at that time, and my walls were filled with pictures of all my favorite local race car drivers. I didn't have girls or pictures of rock bands on my wall; I had race cars. Every day, I would use one of the pictures from the race program and draw one of my favorite drivers. Always liked Ron Blackmer, Skip Furlow, Rich Gardner, Ron Davies, Dave Scott, and Dick Barton because those guys always put on a show. Chub Frank was a local hero who followed the stars' circuit. Everybody was always proud of him as he ran with the big boys and won a lot. He would occasionally come home to run with the locals and usually found his way to the front. You couldn't beat the guy at Raceway 7 many nights, as he would always find that high side and just fly around somebody in the late moments of the race. These guys were my heroes when I was younger, so it would be no surprise that this sport might be part of my future.

I organized a "race day" at our local pub, and about fifteen cars showed up. That place was packed, and I know the bar owner made a lot of money. Soon after that race day, the bar owner asked, "Do ya think we could do another one?" It was a fun day, as many of the local stars brought their cars out, plus we had raffles and sold T-shirts. We did have other race days, but none of them were as successful as the first event.

Around that time, I was also playing on the computer, learning how to draw race cars with a new art program. I got the computer when I graduated from college with the help of OVR. OVR would help with any equipment that would aid in a job or make your house more accessible, such as computers, vehicles, ramps, and lifts. I messed around with the computer for a while and saw that it had a drawing program, so I started playing around with it. Well, it took me a while to draw the cars because I had to do it layer by layer and then put the main drawing to the front. When the project was finished, I had a race car on the screen. Then I had to design the background so it would look flashy. I looked at some of the professional's work and did the best I could to get something close. T-shirts by the big companies were expensive at that time, and most of the locals just wanted something to get quickly and in a certain order. That is where I came in. I'd take a week or so to draw the car, design the decals, and put the sponsors on the back. I'd send them a copy, and they would review it and then let me know if any changes were needed. Then I'd have to print out the color of each layer and send it to a printer in Illinois that would put them together and print them on T-shirts. I would get a box of shirts in two or three days, then take them out to the people, and they'd pay me. They were not as good as the professionals, but it took me a lot of time, and I had a lot of pride in my work.

This was right around the time I got my first teaching job, had the pizza shop, and organized a successful race car show at Butch's Pub. I was talking to one of the drivers, a friend of mine, Dwayne. They had a race car and weren't going to be racing next year, so we discussed getting a race team together. After deciding to go for it, we went searching for a car. We drove around back roads and then finally found a car sitting out in the back of someone's garage. We bought the car for four hundred bucks and then dragged it back to the garage. After removing the body, we were disappointed to find out the frame was in poor shape, so we had to find a better frame. We talked with a buddy of Dwayne's, and he had a frame with a roll cage already installed on it sitting at his house. We dragged it out to the garage and started to assemble it. While we were building the car, I took out a loan for $1,500, bought a 400 Chevy block, and then took it to a motor builder who had the parts to turn it into a 383 stroker engine. Everything in the motor was bone stock. We just wanted it balanced. When a motor is balanced, the motor spins freely with no drag, in simple terms. We bought four racing springs and replaced them with the original stock springs, and then we put a racing fuel cell in the car. We had enough money to buy three Hoosier racing tires and then got two street tires from Fink's Tire for sponsorship. We put the street tire on the left front because that tire does the least in racing, and the other three on the rest of the corners. We painted the frame bright orange because it's my favorite color and then the body panels black. Then I went to Cooper's to help come up with a design for the car. The car's look consisted of orange and black with just a hint of yellow. The damn thing looked good, as I always thought black cars stood out on a racetrack. At Cooper's, we produced a clean design that would stick out while the car was on the track. He did all the artwork on the computer and then printed out a final look. From that point, a cutter cuts out the vinal to the size of your car, and then transfer paper is applied to the sticker so you can apply it to the race car. Cooper came to the garage and showed us how to put the stickers on because we had no fuckin' clue what to do. I did buy five chrome rims because they have a beautiful shine that makes any car look sharp, especially in black and orange. That night, Dad and I went out to look for a trailer to haul the race car and finally found one that another fellow racer had in his backyard.

Dad asked, "Are you really gonna do this, or I'm not gonna get involved?"

And I was like, "Well, the car is ready. We just need this trailer because we're gonna race."

At that time, Raceway 7 was getting about forty-five of the best pure stocks around. Only twenty-four cars made the feature, so it was going to be tough for our first night to go out to even make the field, let alone beat them. Dad kept saying, "Those guys are flying around there. You're probably going to look like a damn joke."

I replied, "I know we looked like a bunch of rednecks, but I'm telling you, we put together a nice-looking car, I always preached. The first thing you must have is a great-looking car, and then try to get that girl to run fast."

We didn't know what the motor was going to do because it wasn't a true racing motor, just balanced with stock engine parts and a bigger cam. We had it ready to go. Time to see what we got.

Heat races are usually eight laps, and the top four make a redraw for your feature starting spot. In our heat, there were ten cars, and we ended up finishing second, which put us in the draw for the feature. We drew a fifth-place starting spot, and the hot dog of the track was starting on the pole. I'm  sure we raised my dad's eyebrows a bit, just finishing second in the heat race. I was very happy because I really wasn't expecting to run that well.

We started fifth in the feature and started passing cars just after the green flag flew. Dwayne went by fourth place and then got by third place and began to pressure the second-place car. After an inside move, Dwayne passed the second-place car and then started to run down the leader. As the race went on, he pressured the first-place car, continuously trying to get by him. With two laps to go, he got beside the leader, coming out of turn two, but spun out and was hit by another car right in the rear, ending it. I was smiling like a kid in a candy store, and Dad sure didn't have a lot to say. I was pretty hooked, as racing is like a drug because you just can't get it out of your system.

I had $150 in my checking account, so I went to a fellow racer who had a rear end and bought it for $145, leaving me $5 in my checking account. We mainly raced one night a week at Raceway 7 in Ohio. That car was fast, as we should have won eight races that year. But what did we actually win? One. We were leading eight races when a tire would always pop off the bead. We had three damn racing tires, so we always had to rotate the three in different locations just to keep them fresh. The beads on these rims were not very thick, so the tire would always slide off. I don't believe we were allowed to run beadlocks at the time, so that was the reason we had so many tires fall off the rim. A beadlock allows you to bolt the tire to the rim so it is locked down in one place. We had to just keep rotating tires and hope for the best. We finally won one night at Christmas in July. We were so fast all season and ran up front with that stock 383 stroker motor. A lot of teams would always say you can't win with a stock motor, but I'm telling you, we did for only $1,500. After that race, we went to the bar and played Queen's "We Are the Champions." We danced around celebrating like we won $1,000,000. I know, my dad was shocked to shit, as he didn't think we were going to be worth a damn. We did all this with three racing tires and a stock 383 engine.

We did go to Mercer Raceway once and started eighteenth in the feature, and then we raced all the way up to third, but somebody spun him out. It was too late in the race to gain any more spots, so we finished toward the back, but it sure didn't reflect how the car ran. We also went to Tri-City one time but only had one set of gears, and the ones we had in the car were not good enough for that big track. We started tenth in the heat race and ended up third. During the feature, we started seventh and raced to a third-place finish. Boy, that motor was screaming that night, and I thought she was going to blow up, but the motor held up for the whole season. If we had had the right gear, Dwayne would have smoked them. We finished eighth in points that first year at Raceway, with an average of forty cars showing up every week, even though we missed a few nights early in the season.

My cousin Sam took a lot of pictures of our cars during those early years. He was the guy behind most of the pictures that hung on my wall today. Sam was from Slippery Rock, so he'd come up and then spend the night hanging out with us during the weekend. One day, we were going by the water tower by the fairgrounds, going into Meadville to get something to eat. We passed the tower and then headed around the curve that went toward Meadville. They had just recently paved the road, and there was a six-inch berm along the edge. While driving, the edge of my tire caught that berm, ripping my hand out of the wheel and then my hand out of my brake. I couldn't steer or stop it, so the van took off across a ditch, around a huge tree, back through the ditch, across the road, then into somebody's driveway. Luckily, I pushed the brake right before we ran into his garage, putting it in park. I looked to my right and then saw my cousin Sam staring straight ahead with the cigarette in his mouth. He didn't look at me at all, just straight ahead, reaching his fingers up to take a final puff of his smoke. He pulled it out and, looking straight ahead, said, "I'll check the tires."

Unbelievably, we didn't hurt anything on that truck. And we went through a damn Baja Zone. How do I live through these things?

During the winter, we bought many new parts for the car, including new bushings. We thought the car was going to fly, just kicking everyone's ass next season. We now had a beadlock for the right rear and took the motor to the builder to have it freshened up and ready for the upcoming season. We raced almost the entire year with that motor but couldn't get oil to the lifters. The car would only run about three laps, and then the engine light would come on. We didn't blow the motor up, but it wouldn't run long enough to see if the car would handle it. After having this problem most of the season, we got the oil problem fixed and started to run more laps, showing us the car handled like a dump truck. It wouldn't get ahold of the track, sliding up in every corner. Everybody was passing us, giving Dad a reason to say we "suck." We checked just about everything in the car but couldn't figure it out. Then we checked out those damn bushings. They were so damn stiff they wouldn't let the card flex. I bought high-dollar bushings that kept a streetcar stable but gave our race car handling problems. We then went to the parts store and bought cheaper bushings to put back in the car. There were only a few races left in the season, so we went out there and blew the doors off everybody. But did we win? Hell no. The car came to rest three feet from the checkered flag. I went to the fence, looked at Dwayne, and he just put his hands up in the air and then shrugged his shoulders like he didn't know what happened. We got to the pits and found out the battery cable had come off. Probably one of the things we checked on the car while figuring out our damn problem, but we didn't tighten it right. Never did get a win that year. Racing kicks you right in the nuts. Just when you think you got it figured out, you don't know shit. I've learned that just because you buy better parts doesn't mean that your race car will run faster.

That next year, we moved up to the E-mod class and purchased a brand-new chassis. The E-mod class has a tubular chassis built onto a frontal car frame. Everybody knows that buying a new car can be quite expensive, and we didn't have a lot of  money, so we bought everything piece by piece. We put it together in a cold garage that a friend of Dwayne's let us use during those winter months. We'd get a part, hurriedly put it on, and then sit there looking at each other. I'd get paid, buy a few more parts, and then place them on the race car to get it done because the season was approaching fast.

We were supposed to race that Friday night, so we tested the car down the road that Thursday night. Dwayne was flying down that road, turning the motor to max rpm, with a dust cloud bursting behind him. The sound of that motor purring gave me an instant chub, and you could see the car coming up over the hill, whizzing by me. When he went to hit the brakes, the car didn't stop. He went flying through the intersection and onto the next road across from it. Good thing that road didn't come to a T, or we would have destroyed that car. After Dwayne pulled back into the driveway, we saw the master cylinder was leaking around a fitting. I went to the parts store to get a couple of fittings to replace the bad one, but it continued to leak. We had to purchase a race fitting the next day so we could race that night.

Everything finally worked, so Saturday night, we towed to Hickory Speedway, located near Slippery Rock, Pennsylvania. I've seen races there before but never raced my cars there. During our heat race, Dwayne took it easy running in the back of the field to test the car's performance and then said, "Everything's good to go. Let's race." He started at eighteen, and you could tell that practice time was over for that boy. He quickly moved into the top ten and then started getting closer to the lead cars. He got around the fifth-place car and tried to pass the fourth-place car on the high side but lost it, slamming into the wall with the back of the car. First night out, and the rear of the car was bent about a foot to the right. I thought it was all over because I had a new car that was now just a boat anchor. Luckily, all we had to do was put it on the frame machine and bend it back. That was a learning year, and we knew that the motors we were running were just not strong enough to run bigger tracks. The stock 383 stroker motor was good for a fourth-, fifth-, or sixth-place finish, but we could not compete for the lead. That's when Dwayne had to leave.

Dwayne took a job working for a company that installed bleachers for NASCAR and informed us he could no longer drive for me. Right around that time, a local driver mentioned his car wasn't finished yet, so I decided to let him run my car until his car was  completed. Jim lived fifteen minutes from my house, so working on the car would be within a reasonable distance. We loaded the car up, packed all our equipment into the truck, and headed to Jim's garage. Jim was very particular, as his cars were always sharp and very detailed. I felt the same way about my car. It was well-prepared and presentable for sponsors.

After a few nights of bullshit, I said, "You have a car, and I have a car. Let's team up and go racing." I was not one to sit around and chat. I just wanted to race. Raceway 7 was a three-eight-mile track, and my little 383 stroker was just not good enough to win. Jim had a bigger motor in his car, so we ran his car on the larger tracks and mine on the smaller tracks. If the track was small, my car could run with anybody. We went to Mercer Raceway toward the end of the year, and Jim got his first win in my car with an exciting last-lap pass. The track got one lane toward the end, but the leader screwed up and drove out of the preferred grove, letting Jim sneak by to the inside for the win. That was our first win together and my first win as an E-mod owner. I believe that was Jim's first career win in any race car. The funny part of that win came when the picture of our win was posted in the paper, and Jim's suit had a rip in the crotch, and you could see his underwear through the suit. We laughed about it, and Jim decided to get himself a new racing suit for next year.

While racing my car at Raceway 7 one night, Jim was passing cars with ease on the high side of every corner. A car spun toward the infield and then back up the track in front of Jim. Jim hit that driver full throttle, destroying the car. I heard my pit crew guy saying, "I think it's just bent a little bit." The frame was bent in a Z shape, and the only thing actually good on the car was the radiator. We have no insurance in racing. If you destroy it, you buy another one. Race cars are very expensive, so I started saving money to purchase another car for next season. We raced his car the rest of the year and had good finishes, but things were going to get much better after a new car was added to the stable.

The next year, we purchased a Pierce race car because it was hot modified at that time. That car was one badass-looking race car. With Jim's body design, those black, orange, and white decals, that car just popped from the stands. Kids usually pick nice-looking cars as their favorite, and it worked for us because Jim found his future wife during an autograph session while her kid stopped down to get his signature. Raceway 7 had a lot of tough modifieds. Jim got quite a few wins at that track because that car would really come out of the corners and pass guys on the low side.

One funny moment happened when Tom and Joe were getting the car out of the garage to wash it. We pulled the car out and placed a rock underneath the front tire to keep it from rolling. Out of the corner of my eye, I could see the car start to move and roll toward the hill. Tom grabbed the wheel, and the car turned to the left, sending it down into a pile of old rusted equipment. Something put a hole in the side of the door and a dent in the front bumper. Jimmy always liked his car to look immaculate, so we were horrified. We got the four-wheeler to help pull the car back into the garage and fix the damage. I don't think Jim ever noticed it because it was a race car, and the scrapes you get from weekly racing blended in. We also ran really well at Tri-City Speedway, as Jim picked up two or three wins there. Everybody down there ran Pierce cars because not many other chassis could even run with those cars.

It was right around that time that I bought a second Pierce car to add to our table. Jim drove it a few times but didn't really like it. I owned this entire car, and Jim had money invested in the old car. With two cars, I wanted to race more and travel to different tracks. I understand guys have to work, please girlfriends, and stuff like that, but all I wanted to do was race as much as we could. I put a driver named Matt in my car that night at Tri-City Speedway, and Jim drove the other car. During the feature, Matt passed Jim in the closing laps of the race and finished third. Jim was upset because he was racing for the points at Tri-City while Matt got out, saying, "Hey, Scott told me to drive the thing, so I did." Matt told me after the race, "I'll race anywhere you want to race, any day or place." There was an argument after the race, where tempers were high. In my mind, I knew this would never work. So I took one car, then Jim and I parted ways.

A funny moment racing at Sharon Speedway one night. Jim's dad never liked us racing anywhere but Raceway 7 because he was always worried about the points. We went to Sharon Speedway for a big race for modifieds. Jim was running a hell of a race in third, trying to pass for second. Somehow, there was contact, and then we got involved with a big wreck. After they towed the car into pits, Jim's dad said, "Loaded it up, we're done. No more Raceway 7 points championship for us." We all argued that Jim ran a good race, having a great chance to win. His dad argued with us for a while and then said he was leaving. So he picked up his lunch box and said, "I'm walking home." After about an hour, he came crawling back with his ass dragging, saying, "I need a ride home." Leroy always said we were done after every wreck we had. But we always had the car ready for the next week. I had a lot of fun with the Frontzes.

Toward the end of the year, we towed to a big race at Sharon Speedway that was paying $800 to win, a lot for the modifieds at that time. Matt drove a hell of a race, catching the dominator of modifies, Randy Hall. Matt was all over him  with five laps remaining and repeatedly dove low, forcing Randy lower in order to protect his position. In the final corner, Matt drove around the outside of him and won the damn thing. We had a crew of two fifteen-year-olds, a twelve-year-old, a handicapped, and one hell of a diver. Do you think we were excited about next year? Let's turn the page and find out.

The next year, we went on a tear and won twenty-five races at multiple tracks. What was the reason for our success? Bob Pierce  made the cars that everyone had such great success with on many local tracks. Tri-City had an open practice where Bob Pierce came to help all the drivers who ran his cars. We towed down to practice and tried a few things. After a few runs, we switched the springs in the front of the car, and boy, did that thing take off. The car would turn so nice in the corners and lay over on the right front tire. That car would get so much traction at just about every track we raced and found victory lane twenty-five times at five different tracks. We won about ten races at Tri-City Speedway that year and the two big races at the end of the season. You could start anywhere from first to twelfth with the luck of a pill draw, but it didn't matter where we started. That car could get lower than anybody else's car and find its way to the front before twenty laps were done. Just about everyone in the field was racing a Pierce car there, but they couldn't figure out what we were doing. We had a hell of a crew, family, and driver, but it was just something that we found in that practice session that set the car apart.

We did have a bump in the road toward the end of the season though. Drivers were tired of being passed by us, so one spun out the car. A driver behind us hit the front of the car and bent it about a foot to the right. I remember sitting in pits, seeing teams walk by smiling, waving, and laughing about our misfortune, believing they ended our season. I remember yelling to one guy, "We're gonna come back and win every single race, including the big ones too."

They said, "Yeah, right."

We took it to a frame machine to bend it back to its standard measurement and put the motor back in so we were ready for the next week. We not only won the last four races but also the $800 win on Friday and the $1,000 to win on Saturday. While heading down to victory lane, Tom's face planted his head into the ground as we crossed the track. He didn't get his hands down in front of him and scraped his face across the ground. You could hear the crowd moan, "Oohhhh."

"Big T," as we called him, took it in stride and smiled during our pictures. Again, it was not bad for a twelve-year-old, two fifteen-year-olds, a handicapped, and an awesome driver.

Around this time, I started designing the stickers and then administering them to the cars. For customers, I had to create the graphics they wanted and then show them proof of their finished product. It would take me about a week to come up with a design and a weekend to cut the vinyl. I used a graphic cutter to cut the vinyl to be put on the car. Okay, I was not even close to being as good as a seasoned veteran, but I made the cars look pretty good. The cutter I purchased was not the top of the line, but it was a cheap model that would make mistakes if the graphic was too big. I'd have to purchase more vinyl if it fucked up during a run, then I didn't have another piece in the size I needed. Boy, that cutter pissed me off. I'd order vinyl most of the time from a vinyl shop online, but there was a shop in Meadville that would always have more on hand if needed. It only took me ten minutes to drive into town if I screwed shit up. Matt and Tim would always come over to help me because it might take ten hours to cut vinyl for a car.

In those days, you would have four to six layers on a sticker and then show like one-fourth inch of each color just to get the decal right. After you cut the stickers out, you had to put application tape on each sticker so you could later apply them to the car. You had to apply the first layer, second layer, third layer, and then occasionally up to six layers to make a car number. If we started early enough, we could get a car done in a day. If it was our car, we would come back the next day and then button up what wasn't finished the day before. I know we didn't admit it, but it was a strenuous job that took a lot out of us. We needed to invest in a cutter that would save time and money and relieve the stress on our bodies.

After a year of dealing with that shitty cutter, I went out and purchased a much better one. This allowed me to do all our cars and then a couple of our friends' cars too. It saved a lot of money owning your own vinyl cutter because you could be charged $700 to $1,000 or more to do decals for your car. I could purchase the vinyl for about $300, design the car, cut the stickers, and then apply them for no additional charge. In three years, it would only cost you $900 as opposed to about $3,000 if someone else created your sticker package. It was time-consuming, but we loved to do it. When I did my cars, I wanted to use fluorescent colors, giving them a bling-bling look. I wanted it to glow at night so the sponsors were readable from the stands. Don't forget the chrome rims because they add the exclamation point to the look of your race car. I took a lot of pride in my designs and thought many of them were pretty badass.

The next year, Matt wanted to travel a bit more, so we decided to follow the Road Warrior Tour, which consisted of the races in Ohio, West Virginia, and Kentucky. My crew were still just kids at this point, and I was responsible for all actions once we left Pennsylvania. There were times 

when the guys wanted to quit and then have their parents come pick them up and head home. I was like, "You're six hours from home. Suck it up, and get back in the game. Racing is tough. Wins come so infrequently for the hours of work you put into the car." The families did pitch in to help us when the races were closer to home, but days get a little more intense on the road when you're spending long days together, working in the hot midday sun, and getting to a hotel at two in the morning.

One night, the three crew boys, Matt, Tim, and Tom, were heading up the elevator toward our room. On this trip, my brother KC and his future wife Kelly were riding up the Vader with us. We were asking who was sleeping where, and then the youngest, Matt, said, "I'm sleeping with Tits."

Now Kelly, who was top-heavy in the boob department, said, "Mathew, that is so rude."

Matt responded, "What? I'm sleeping with Tom."

What makes this funny? Tom is a tire specialist, so, a.k.a. Tits, Kelly had no idea, but we all did, which made it so funny and a good stress reliever during a long racing trip.

In the garage one week, while working on the car, the boys put me in my new chair. They made a little racetrack out of spare tractor tires so I could turn some laps. I had my old chair there also, so Tom climbed in that thing, and, of course, we had to have a race. We decided to run a twenty-five lapper around our little track. Tom and I were dicing around that track, cutting inside and outside, trying to get an advantage. The chairs were exactly the same, so there was no distinct advantage with either chair. We got down to three laps to go, and I cut to the inside. Tom dove low also, slamming me into the side of the tires and putting my chair on two wheels. My chair teetered on two wheels as I drew closer to the wall, slamming hard to the ground, causing parts to fly everywhere. Tom continued forward, with hard contact with the bench, knocking the light fixture off the wall. Of course, all the crew ran over to try to get me upright. I came out of that big wreck with no bruises or cuts. My new chair did have a little bit of damage on it, but nothing to affect its performance. The funny thing is, there were no winners, as we both had a DQ.

I had to take a personal care attendant with me during the long trips, who luckily didn't have much of a family at home. It was hard at times, but we did it. I took this PC on a two-day race trip, and it was only her second week working for me. She came light, with one bag of clothes and no money. I really didn't care, as she was helping me out, so she just stayed in my room, and I paid for her food. I was cold coming back from the races, so I asked her to put me in the shower to warm up. As I was sitting in there, I had the shits and then told her to put a garbage can under me to catch it. The can filled up with water, letting shit spill all over the shower floor. I truly felt bad for her, being her first week and all, but nothing new to me. I've spread shit through a whole school, so this minor blip was nothing more than a quick chuckle for me. Sometimes, I'd have KC, Tim, or Matt help get me up or throw me in bed. Their mother was a registered nurse, so even if I needed an antibiotic, I could still travel with the team to any event. At that point, gas was cheap, food was cheap, and racing wasn't too expensive. We were having fun on the road and enjoyed testing our team against some of the best drivers of West Virginia, Ohio, and Kentucky.

Our first race was at Elkins Speedway in West Virginia. We've never been to any of these tracks, so we mingled with the drivers who followed the series full-time to find out about tires and possible gear choices. Many asked us where we were from and what we were doing here. We repeatedly said, "We're gonna try to follow the whole series, trying to do something different from previous years." You qualified to find your starting spot in the heat race, timing in with a fifth fastest time out of thirty-plus cars. We ran second in our heat race and then drew a fifth-place start for the feature. There wasn't a lot of passing, remaining in fifth place the whole race, but with laps winding down, we hit a hole, breaking one of the four-bar rods. Yes, it sucks, but in racing, you are never a winner till you pass the checkers and make sure your car is of weight. I've lost races in both situations, making it a long ride home and kicking myself in the nuts because of something we did or didn't do in the car.

Tyler County is one badass racetrack. When you first see it, you'd think go-karts race around that track, then see a dirt late model flinging dirt around the top of it and totally shit your drawers. There's nothing like being two feet from a car going eighty miles per hour inches from the wall. Matt quickly figured out a fast way around the track, qualifying in the top five. He finished first in his heat race, then pulled a third starting spot for our feature. Matt quickly got to second and then ran there for the rest of the race. We should have had a little more gear in the car, as it was lagging a little bit coming off the corners, but I didn't think we had any gear that small. The other teams started talking to us a little bit more, believing we were serious about racing the tour. It was cool having some of the older guys come down to speak with us, telling us some of their secrets and what times to run a certain tire. We towed four hours home, discussing how our first weekend on the tour was a success. We ran with some of Ohio's best modifieds and ran very well, especially on tracks we have never raced on.

The next weekend, we towed six hours to Chillicothe Speedway in southern Ohio, where sixty-five modifieds filled the pits that  night. We qualified sixth, which put us on the pole for the heat race. We won the heat race going away, putting us on the pole for the feature. We talked to one of the elders modified stars, asking him, "What tire should we run, the hard or the medium?"

He said with a straight face, "Well, if you're going to start near the front, run a medium. If you're going to be in the back, run a harder tire because you're going to run harder to get to the front."

We put on medium Hoosier tires and then ran twenty-nine laps up front till the last lap, when a hard-charging driver went around the outside of us, beating us to the checkered flag. Yeah, I was disappointed, but we just ran great against sixty-five of the best modifieds in Ohio. Then I heard over the loudspeaker that the winner was disqualified because his car was light on the scales. I have been there and done that, folks. Even though you hate to win that way, a $1,000 check with first place stamped on the check still has your name on it. This was the first win of the season, with Willard Speedway in Kentucky and then Brush Creek Speedway in Ohio next on the schedule.

We loaded up and drove home for six hours, gossiping about being second in Road Warrior Tour points.

The next week, we headed to Willard Speedway in Kentucky. After driving for about six hours, we arrived in this little town that had about one streetlight and a little county store. We stopped and asked for directions, and then a young lad directed us toward the racetrack. After driving about three miles, we followed a fellow racer to the track that was behind a cornfield. The facilities might have been redneck, but the racetrack was very nice. Matt qualified second and won our heat race. After drawing a sixth-place starting position, Matt quickly got to fifth on the first lap, passing for fourth a lap later. Matt ran in fourth place for most of the race, and then the tire started to smoke. Our left rear tire went flat with three laps to go, ending the great run our team had. Somehow, the birdcage flipped, pushing the tire into the back of the frame, finally cutting our tire. We didn't really know why the birdcage flipped, so we changed the tire, loaded up the car, and then headed to Brush Creek Racing Complex the next night.

Brush Creek was a racetrack that had three corners, like no other track we've ever seen before. Cars that raced weekly definitely had an advantage on where to run on that track. Matt struggled a bit in qualifying, ending up near the back in the heat race. We finished fifth in our heat race, failing to make the pill draw. Matt started fifteenth in the feature, racing to about twelfth place when the car started to smoke. He pulled the car into the pits, checked the engine, and then found out we had a broken piston. That was the end of a pretty shitty weekend. We didn't know how bad the motor was, but we knew we had to take it out of the car and get it checked by our motor builder. We were now down to our last motor, so the team decided to call off running the rest of the modified tour. I didn't know how everybody else felt, but to me, it was a relief for us to travel less, racing closer to home. To run on the road, you have to be organized, have enough spare parts in the trailer, and hope your team has very few mechanical problems. Hey, we tried it and ran well with Ohio's best modifieds, getting a big win at Chillicothe Speedway.

We raced around our local tracks the rest of the year, getting seven wins. Something was just missing on that car from what we had the previous year, and we could never put a finger on it. Matt still got the car to the front, but it sure didn't seem to handle or dig off the bottom like it did the year before. The only thing we changed on that car was the cracked  upper frame rail. We replaced it during the offseason, but that car didn't seem to have as much left rear drive in it, and it never raced the same way to me. Matt started racing his late model again toward the end of the year, deciding to put more time into his operation.

We parted ways on friendly terms because we knew that his real dream was racing dirt late models. That ended our most successful stint in racing, winning around thirty-three races at numerous tracks around the area. We sold that car at the end of the year, placing an order for a new Pierce modified for next year. At this point, we didn't even know who the hell the driver was going to be yet.

During the offseason, I got a call from Bobby, a local hot shoe that won a lot of races in the pure stocks and modifieds. He said, "Go ahead, put my name in the hat to drive your car." After talking for a while, we contacted Bobby to tell him he got the ride for next year. We decided to race all three local tracks in the area, where Bobby won about thirteen heat races that year.

You can draw a pill anywhere from first to twelfth place for the feature, and 95 percent of the time, we drew a fuckin' twelve every damn race. Bobby would race his way up to third or fourth every night, but he could never get a good pill and then win with that car. The last straw came during a big race at Erie Speedway. We won our heat race again and then drew the twelfth starting spot for the feature. At the start of the race, Bobby would pass three or four cars, and then the yellow flag would come out, putting him back to twelfth again. We would have another start, pass three or four cars, and then another yellow would come out. They kept putting us back to eleventh or twelfth, passing one car at a time through numerous cautions until the feature came to an end. We finished about seventh place after all the laps had been completed. I wheeled down to the car and then yelled, "We're selling this fuckin' car, getting out of this division, and getting a crate late model!" A week later, we sold the modified and both motors. Then we went to Rob Blair's house to buy one of his late models. Our new adventure was about to begin.

I always wanted to own a late model, and with the cost of the crate engine, I could finally do what I wanted to do my whole life. The crate motors cost about $5,000 at the time. With all the accessories, you could put a whole crate motor together for about seven grand. I bought the car from Blair's for $10,000 and then brought the motor right to Rob's place. They put the motor in the car, and then Rob set up the car with his magi-cal touch. I think that man is one of the best at setting up a race car. Rob's cars were always fast right out of the gate and then always ran up front. At the time, we were racing under the fast track series, where you got points for all your feature finishes. You could race at all your weekly tracks, acuminating points toward the Fastrak championship. We won a lot of races that year, putting us neck and neck with Rob's son, Max Blair, for the fast track series point lead. It was nip and tuck all the way to the end. At one point, we reached about the max number of points. Bobby tried pulling a fast one on the Blairs by towing down to Dog Hollow Speedway. Our local tracks were finished, so we headed south to race at a track to get more points. I was telling Bobby, "We should probably tell the Blairs we're heading down to race for more points." He didn't tell them till we about pulled in the place, pissing the Blairs off. I think we had a gentleman's agreement because we were friends, plus competitors. We won that night, taking the lead in the points, but lost some friends. The Blairs also started towing down every weekend. Max ended up winning the championship by about two points.

We used to do a lot of the tour-ing races, with many tracks around the region. Every race was usually two or three hours away, with about twelve guys that followed the series. Max was definitely the hot dog of the series, but we also won our share. We had a series race at Dog Hollow Speedway, where Bobby passed a guy late in the race to win the $1,200. We left the racetrack on cloud nine, talking about our next adventure, a national race paying $10,000 to win at Wytheville Speedway in Virginia. We drove seven hours watching every episode of Beavis and Butthead, feeling like we were on top of the world. We had $1,200 in our hand, heading south to kick ass and take names like we did the night before. To get on the track, you drive down a big hill and then park in the center of it.

The place was fuckin' huge. It sure wasn't a small little track like the one we had just won on the night before. We put gears in the car that work well on a big racetrack, then qualified seventy-eighth out of eighty cars. Bobby couldn't pass a damn car in the heat race and was going to start twenty-third in B-main the next day. Sometimes, you just get your ass kicked, need to just put your tail between your legs, and get the hell home. I've always learned when you think your hot shit, there's always somebody better out there knocking at the door, ready to tear it down. Never brag unless there is a damn good reason too. Humility, karma, etc.

Toward the end of that season, things started to get heated between driver and crew. Bobby said, "He wasn't gonna race anymore if we kept the Lattas on as a crew." Lattas didn't want Bobby to be a driver, or they were going to leave. I'm a lover,  not a fighter, and I didn't really know what to do at the time. I was the one who had money invested and had to make the hard decision to keep the driver because we were so close to the top of the points. The winner got $10,000, and I was never rich, so that was a lot of money. The Lattas had been racing with me pretty much my entire dirt track career, with our families so close. It was a difficult decision that I had to live with at the time. We finished the year second in the points, making $3,000. Was it worth it? Probably not. We should have come up with a better solution, but that's the choice I made, and I had to live with it.

We had a lot of fun with Bobby during those years though. We had a race at Mckean County at the end of the year, and we were taking a travel trailer with us. Everyone had to work first and then headed to the track, getting there pretty late. Another camper had already taken his spot, so Bobby had to back our camper beside him, running over the man's water hoses that were hooked to his trailer. Bobby asked the guy to disconnect his hoses so he wouldn't run over the top of them. The camper bitched and moaned about us getting there late and then about running over his hoses. We got our trailer set up and headed to a bar in Bradford, Pennsylvania. These boys could party till the last call, have a great time, and close down the bar. McDonald's would not serve walk-ins, so the only thing that was open was the drive-through. They said we needed a vehicle in order to order there, so I drove my goddamn chair to the window, getting our food. The servers gave us a pissed-off glare as we headed back to my van. After we got back to the track, Bobby unhooked the guy's waterline and then pissed in it. Not the nicest thing to do, but that guy was such an asshole.

Next came our Fastrak banquet in Greenville, Pennsylvania. It seemed to be dragging out, so we had another driver pick up our points check, as we headed to Headliners strip joint. Four of us were crammed into our ambulance, driving about ten miles per hour on snow-covered roads. When we arrived, a bouncer came and yelled out, "Oh, thank God you're here. We have a girl that broke her leg."

We all laughed and then said, "We're not the damn ambulance. This is our tow vehicle."

It was close to my birthday, so Bobby bought me a lap dance. The girl took me to a back room and then started dancing seductively in front of me. She did a cartwheel, straddled my lap, then her ass cheek hit my joystick, sending my wheelchair across the room, slamming into the wall. I was yelling at her, "Get off, get off!" A bodyguard came over to help her off my lap. You could see where my tires burned a rubber streak into the floor as I told the dancer, "That's probably the best ride you ever had." She gave me a wink as a new story was born.

Toward the end of the year, Bobby said racing was getting too much, becoming a strain on his family. He decided he didn't want to race the car the next year, so I called up my buddy Dwayne, and he decided to drive the car. For most of the year, Dwayne struggled with the car, picking up one win. What a crazy day that was. We were heading down to Tyler County Speedway, which was three and a half hours away. While towing past Pittsburgh, we had two tires blow on the ambulance and then had to pull over. Then two crew guys went to look for a place to buy tires, leaving us stranded in the parking lot for about five hours. Then, at six, they finally returned with the ambulance, which had two brand-new tires. Instead of heading down to Tyler County, we hooked up the trailer and then raced back to Mercer Speedway. We pulled in the right as the heat races were starting, unloaded the car, hit the track in last place, and then quickly raced himself into a transfer position. We picked a second-place pill, and then before lap one was completed, he had the lead and never looked back. That win actually just paid for the two tires we purchased for the ambulance. We got one win that year, just never having the mojo we did in the pure stocks, and after a blown motor, I was ready to find another driver.

During this time, we kept the car at one of my sponsors' garages, Mitchell's Milk Hauling. Gambling is just like racing; you spend a lot of money, getting little in return. My grandma was the first one that got me into gambling. It started off with going to local games of bingo, and then we headed to the casino after I turned twenty-one. Luckily, my best buddy was Michael Mitchell, who was a gambler too. We'd always head up to Erie and then put forth an even amount of money. Then whatever we won, we'd split. We've won quite a few jackpots during our times up there, but never anything to write home about. One night, he was playing blackjack at the tables when this beautiful tanned Brazilian girl walked up to the table. She was wearing a real tight-chested outfit, with a really short miniskirt. Just beautiful. She sat down beside Mike and then asked him how to play this game. The funny part? Mike had a chew in his mouth and hadn't spit for like twenty minutes. Then she asked him again, "How do you play this game?" When he tried to speak, nothing but "Wa, wa, wa" came out. She looked at him wide-eyed, then got up, and took off. He looked at me, spit in a cup, and then said, "I sounded like a goddamn retard."

I said, "Yes, you blew that chance of talking to that beautiful girl." He sounded like he had a mouth full of shit, but boy was that funny.

Two great things happened at that point. I got John Volpe as my driver, who had a lot of skill in the late model division, and then the car went back to the Lattas, who agreed to wrench on the car for the upcoming season. They talked to their parents and then agreed to bring my car back to their garage. I was so happy to hear that because these guys were the best at getting the car ready, and I truly missed my second family. We didn't tiptoe into the season, racing three nights a week, every single weekend. John would drive down from New York, meet us at Raceway 7 on Friday night, then stay in Lattas' camper on Friday and Saturday nights, and then head home after the races on Sunday. We went to Sharon Speedway on Saturday nights and then, lastly, to Erie Speedway on Sunday. We raced till about two in the morning, returned home, slept a bit, got the car ready to go, and headed on to the next track on the schedule. Racing is so damn demanding, taking up every ounce of your free time if you want to run up front. It is a lifestyle that you have to damn near love because it becomes your second job. John was a good-looking kid. He'd always had his hot babe coming out of that trailer in the mornings every weekend. I loved it because she sat beside me when we towed the race car down to the road. It was always nice to have that gorgeous babe by my side, even though she was Big John's. John was a spitfire. At Dog Hollow Speedway, a driver slammed John into a Yuke tire, pretty much destroying the front of the car. John went after the boys in the pits. There was a lot of yelling going on between the teams, but John kept his cool, knowing who he had backing him. What help was I going to be? I guess I could have taken out a few ankles and toes, but that's about it.

During our eighty-race slate, we blew a motor Friday night at Raceway 7. I left the races early to try to find a motor somewhere in the local area. Good friend and sponsor Ed Maloney gave me a check and then said, "Go get another motor." I called John, telling him there was a crate motor located up by Niagara Falls. There was a big race at State Line Speedway that night, so we wanted to attend it. John said, "Yes, let's go for it." It took us about two hours to get up there, get the motor, and then another half hour to locate the dealership. We gave him the check, put the motor in the back of the van, and then headed back to John's place. We took a side street to get to the main road, which was almost straight down. After I got to the bottom of it, I stopped at a stop sign, and then the motor slid up, hitting us in the back of John's seat and the back of my chair. We put something underneath the crate to keep the motor from sliding and then headed home. We got back to the garage to see that the Lattas already had the other motor out and were waiting for us to put this one in. We got the motor in the car and then headed to the racetrack at about six thirty. Once at the track, we had two guys adjusting the lifters on the motor to get it ready to race. We didn't get done in time to make our heat races, but Franny let us tag the field in the twenty-seventh place. John drove that damn thing all the way up to fifth place before getting taken out by a lapped car. Sure seems like when the chips are down, you always have your best performance that night. Even though we ended up finishing thirteenth, we had a great run to the front.

We were at Stateline Speedway one night, with John leading the super late model feature in his own car. A lapped car kept blocking John, so he nudged the driver, spinning him out. The flagman sent John to the tail of the field, which then sent John's dad, Pete, into a fiery debate 
with the flagman. Crew guys flew out of the stands, pulling the flagman from the stand and then rolling around on the ground in front of the boisterous crowd. I always called Pete "Saprano" because his

family looked like the mob rolling around on that track. John's mother was a teacher who was so soft-spoken. I remember her sinking into the bleachers, trying to hide while her family wrestled the flagman in a free-for-all. Would have loved to have been a fly on the wall at their house after the races. John was a great little racer, but he wanted to get back to his own team at season's end, returning to his own dirt late model. I always loved watching that little shit race, always racing tough. We raced about eighty races that year, totally getting his money's worth. I don't remember all the wins we had, but it was quite a few.

Once John left, I had an open ride for somebody. Matt had just completed his first year of racing crate late models and did very well. We raced both cars out of the Lattas' garage, so I didn't have to look very far to find a driver. We decided to team up, racing both cars, one at each track. Matt was always tough at Raceway 7 on Friday nights, plus one of the top dogs at Sharon Speedway on Saturday nights. On Sunday, if everything turned out well on the previous nights, we would go to Erie Speedway occasionally. We basically lived in that garage, ate in that garage, and, a lot of times, slept in that garage. Even though we mainly raced two nights a week, we would be at the garage five or six nights out of the week. I'd bring food one weekend, and then their mom and dad would feed us the next. That garage was my home away from home. Look what those boys have become, just turning wrenches with me in their younger years, to becoming men, starting families, and owning their own race teams.

Matt picked up his first win in my car at Sharon Speedway. He battled up front the entire race, passing the leader with about five laps to go. I was so proud of that boy. I think he felt like he had carried a torch 100 miles, then finally handed it to me.

"I got one for you, White Hat!" screamed his smile. Matt grew up racing at Sharon Speedway, liking it the most. The track seemed to get single file as the years went by, as other drivers must have agreed because they got fewer cars, finally dropping the division. We did still race there occasionally when the Rush Series had touring races, but they're not weekly like they used to be. I remember when you would get forty cars a night, racing very hard just to make the starting field. The top drivers from the area would show up weekly, dicing their crate late models from back to front and vice versa. Boy, what a feeling it was to just run well with that group of drivers. Then we moved on to Eriez Speedway, which I believed you could pass the easiest on, where Matt got one of his biggest Fastrak Series wins. He won the race, passing hot shoe Mike Pegler, then holding off series champ Max Blair. It didn't matter where you started. You could win.

There is one instance that I thought really changed Matt's driving style. We were racing at Eriez Speedway when it came down to the final laps. With two laps to go, three cars were racing down the backstretch, racing for second place. Max Blair was on the outside, with Mike Knight in the middle and Matt low to the inside. Going into turn three, Matt dove underneath both the cars, trying to get bitten on the bottom. Max was coming hard off the top when both cars were racing for the position coming to the flag stand. Now some say that Matt cut off Max or Max didn't brake hard enough, but Max ended up hitting us and then ending up in the wall. During the caution, while Max's car was getting towed to the pits, he walked up and then punched Matt in the helmet. From that point on, I never remember Matt being as aggressive as he was that day. I saw it as two guys just racing hard, with one getting the shit end of the stick. That sometimes happens in racing because nobody wants to intentionally hurt another driver.

Then we went through a very rough stretch. Matt wrecked his car at Sharon Speedway, having to get a new rear clip. A rear clip is where the back half of the car needs to be removed and then replaced what was bent on the car. It costs about $1,400 to put a new rear clip on the car. Matt couldn't drive my car one night, so we called my old driver, Matt Lux, and then headed to a Rush Series race at McKean County Speedway. He got second in the heat and was running about eighth in the feature when a guy slid into the infield and then came back up the track, with Matt hitting him full throttle. They had to flatbed the car into the pits. I remember the flatbed letting the car down, and it sounded like a hunk of junk metal hitting the ground. All the shocks were broken, and the rear of the car was bent, including everything in the front of the car. That car was completely junk.

We had both cars in their grandpa's Marve's garage, one up on the lift, the other on the ground. We didn't know what to do, but I had some money stashed away, so we went to a fellow racer's house to purchase a used Mike Pegher car. We had a touring race that weekend, so we put the motor in the car on the scales and then had it ready for Raceway 7 Friday 

night. Matt almost won the damn thing. He would get to the out-side, the guy, but the bottom groove was better coming out of the corners. Matt pestered him the whole race, finishing a close second. We were very happy with the car, especially with only four days to complete something that takes weeks to accomplish. I was damn proud of everyone for getting the car done and race ready for Friday night.

The next year, Matt got quite a few wins on many different tracks. The most exciting finish, a photo finish win at Raceway 7, pictured to the left. We raced Kyle Zimmerman the whole year trying to win Matt his first championship. It all came down to the last race of the year. With four points separating them, Kyle drew the pole position for the feature, while Matt picked an eight pill. Kyle took off, leading the whole race, while Matt raced all the way to second place. It was a fantastic ending, but not to our liking. Matt did get that championship a few years later, but that loss was a hard pill to swallow. That was our most successful year racing the crate late models. During all these great years, granny Franny and Mike were at all our wins. It was common to see those two smiling in victory lane, taking in the acolytes. Those two drove over two hours every Sunday night to watch us and then headed home after the feature. At ninety years old, that's pretty damn impressive. Rest in peace, Gramma.

Matt got wins at Raceway 7, Stateline Speedway, and Sharon Speedway and then ended the year with a big win on the opening night of a touring race at Tri-City, paying $800 the following year. He then got second the next night to champion Max Blair. Anytime you can race with him, you have to have your shit together because it's going to be a tough race. That was one of our most successful years while racing crate late models. Together, we had achieved everything that I'd wanted to, and then I wanted that next step to cement my career. It was right about then that I wanted to fulfill one of my dreams of owning an actual dirt light model.

Jeff Tregler, my motor builder, called to tell me he had a fresh super late model motor for sale. It cost me $13,000 and made the boys quite excited. The best thing about a crated late model? Just add an 800-horse-power aluminum engine to it, and then it becomes a super late model. You race for more money and against the best dirt track racing has to offer. You burn the tires off much more unless you can handle the extra horsepower. Nothing on the car costs much more, just the shocks and motor. Shocks cost about $4,800, and new motors are anywhere from $30,000 to $50,000. I could never afford a new motor; I just used ones that had been rebuilt. Just starting that motor up in Marvin's garage gave us all a woody. You could feel that motor vibrating in our chests. I'm glad those boys knew what to do with that motor because it cost me a bunch of money, and it was new to us. Every time you move up a division, you have a learning curve. We struggled quite a bit with that car at first, but we got better as the year went on. However, that motor didn't have the horsepower that most did. We struggled mid-pack most nights.

One night, we had a big race at Stateline Speedway, and a rock pierced through the radiator. We did not have a water pressure gauge at the time, so Matt raced till the motor started smoking. He pulled in and, by all accounts, knew the motor was junk. I didn't want my superlight model career to die, so I purchased another motor from a racer in Illinois. That motor just didn't have the ass behind it, the other one did. It did run pretty well on slick tracks but not very well when the track was heavy. If I wanted to do this, I had to step up to the plate. I sent my broken motor to Rhyne Racing Engines in Illinois, and he took the good pieces off that motor, then what still could be used, building me a bigger motor. This motor had 800-plus horsepower, allowing us to run with the big boys. Around that time, Matt got married and started a family of his own. He also had a demanding job that kept him at the business for longer periods of time. He pulled me aside one day, stating he couldn't race as much and was just going to race his crate one night a week.

Like many times before, I now had to find someone to wheel my race car, so the search was on. I now had to pick another driver. Most of the late-model drivers were already racing their own cars, so I needed to find somebody who had the guts to go around the high side when racing somebody on the final lap for a win. I watched a dominant Street Stock driver named Brandon Grooters. He would always go to the front no matter where he started, never following any car. I needed somebody who wasn't going to be afraid of it, put his foot to the floor, and get that car around there. I gave him a call. He agreed, and he ended up being the last driver I ever had. The first night we raced at Hummingbird Speedway. Brandon led most of the race till the car got tight, hit the brakes hard, and then stalled the motor. He went to the back and ended up finishing fourth. The kid definitely put the hammer down and got the most out of that car. You could see he was still very green in the late model. As the year went on, he improved drastically. He got a few seconds and then finished fourth against the best late models in the area at Erie Speedway. His main problem was tearing the spoiler off the car every night. The boy liked the high side, for sure. Hell, he'd tear it off in the heat race, we'd get it fixed, and then he'd tear it off again in the feature. The boy sure could pass cars in the first twenty laps, and then the tires would get hot and lose about five positions in the last five laps. When the year ended, the Lattas kept that car, and I bought a brand-new XR1. During the offseason, Tim informed me he was going to help Matt with his race car for the upcoming season. For the second time in my racing career, I was moving on alone without my boys. This ended a magnificent run where boys became men, and men became dads. Twenty great years of friendship, excitement, heartache, and love of racing. I'll never forget them.

XR1s were the newest chassis in late-model racing. We pieced that car together, and then Brandon put the most beautiful decal job I've ever seen on a late model. The first night, we went to Wayne County Speedway, finishing fifth in the heat race and then starting tenth in the feature. On the very first lap, Brandon got tangled up with a guy and then spun out. He was sent back to twenty-second and then worked his way back up to ninth place. He drove such a smooth race, and the tires came in perfectly. The guy that eventually won the race tried to catch him, but Brandon pulled away late in the race. We knew the tires were working because the car was getting faster as the race went on. It was a great way to start off our season, and the car was in one piece.

Then we had our first race at Eriez Speedway. He started seventh in the feature, quickly racing to third. He was comfortably in third with three laps to go, and then a caution came out. I don't know if the tires heated up or what, but the car seemed very loose coming out of the corners. After a restart, another car got underneath him, causing Brandon to tap the wall and then spin in front of the field. He was drilled by an oncoming driver in the back right corner of the rear. The car never seemed to race the same the rest of the year. It was still very fast, passing a ton of cars, but after twenty laps, the car always seemed to fade. That boy raced hard, just needing time to learn how to feather his foot during the race. We didn't win any races that year, but you sure knew he was in them. One night at Hummingbird, I thought we had that race in the bag, but with two laps to go, a bolt broke that held the brake caliper on, jamming the caliper into the front rotor. The car turned straight into the infield. After the car was towed to the pits, we diagnosed the problem and then shook our heads in disbelief at a problem that never happened. You're never the winner till you cross that checkered flag.

At this point, racing was getting very expensive. I knew the end, for me, was getting closer. We had to drive an hour to work on the car at Brandon's business, where Justin and Theo were now my main pit guys. We really didn't know a whole lot about shocks, but we would go to Lattas every week to test them on their Dyno. After building the car, we moved it closer to home, putting it in my buddy Tom's garage. Brandon would come down once a week to help prepare the car while the rest of us worked on it nightly. Adjusting the shocks throughout the night was our biggest downfall. It was too bad because Brandon was a hell of a driver, getting more confident as he raced nightly, but we could never adjust the car correctly for the feature.

My brother was beside my side for just about all those twenty-four years of racing. I can't think of more than two times that he was not at the races with us. Now while the Lattas were with us, he sure as hell didn't do much. He did say these guys are flying, that guys are flying, or you guys are flying? He would always go up with me, then look at the lineups, and see where everybody was starting. He'd be sure to catch all the heat races, too, and then tell us how the track looked. When I got Brandon as a driver, my brother had to actually do stuff on the crew. He was good at the little things, but when it came to most of the racing things, they told him to get the heck out of the way. I remember this girl came with Brandon one time, so she was head of our crew that night. My brother was dicking around with the air pressure when she told him, "Get the hell out of the way. I'll do it."

My brother took it well, just laughed, and then walked back to the trailer. KC loved racing as much as I did, so it was fun to have him with me all the time.

KC always wanted to drive a race car, but I never put him in mine. While we were young, we'd go to a lot of go-kart tracks where he was a pretty good racer. The funniest time? He was running a track up by Edinboro University, which was a high-banked slick track that raced Sprint cars on it. I could not believe they didn't make people wear helmets because these things were flying around there. While my brother was waiting in line, another fellow racer was wearing a Pat McGuire shirt. Pat McGuire was a good racer around our local area during this time, so we knew this was going to be a race. KC and that gentleman raced around there many laps, going side by side, then spitting cars as they raced to the front. After the flagman stated there were a few more laps left, the other guy dove to the inside, running his tire up over KC's car. They both flew through the outer wall, landing on the outside of the track. The other guy's car was on top of my brother's as he lifted his head to look at me. He had blood pouring out of his nose because he hit his head on the steering wheel. Then he looked at the other guy, saying, "Jesus Christ, Pat, what the hell are you doing?" The guy that owned the track told them both to get the fuck out of there and never come back. Both

men quietly exited the track, with that being the last time we were on those go-karts. Good thing I didn't have KC driving my cars.

We came so close to winning many times. We had a heartbreaker late in the season. We started on the pole with Brandon pulling away after every start, but there were like six cautions during the race, all caused by one guy. On the first lap, the outside pole starter ran over our right front tire and it was slowly losing air. While leading with three laps to go, the car started to bottom out. Brandon spun the car in front of the field, collecting about three cars. If that damn guy wouldn't have spun out every damn lap, we would have won that race. We had a lot of seconds and thirds but never did win a race that was a super late model race. That's the only division I didn't have a chance to get my picture in victory lane. Toward the end of the season, we had motor problems, finally parking the car. I already invested enough in motors and knew the writing was on the wall. I couldn't afford to do this anymore and then told Brandon that I was selling the car. After twenty-four years, I was finally out of racing. Once I sold the truck and trailer, I knew this would never be my pastime again. It brought a tear to my eye because, for more than half my life, I was 100 percent dedicated to this sport. I feel like I was friends with everybody, even during the good and bad times. We all made up after incidents and would help each other if they ever needed a hand. That's what racers did, and I loved being part of that family.

Auto and
Truck Supply
VICTORY LANE

2005 mattlux21.com
Scott Bidwell Motorsports

PERSONAL CARE ATTENDANTS

WHILE LIVING WITH Mom and Dad, I had personal care attendants that had to take care of me. Throughout all the years, I had a gay man, lesbian, swingers, gamblers, racers, and friends who took care of me all those years. I met so many different personalities during that time. I had to share a few memories of the most important moments of my life. I thank and appreciate all the people who have helped me get through my life because I couldn't have done it by myself.

The only time I had a gay man as a personal care tenant was in college. As long as he knew I was straight, I really didn't care, as all I wanted to do was get up. You get real up close and personal doing this job, so you obviously become friends while they work for you. This boy thought like a woman, worried about makeup, fashion, and his fingernails. I always told him that was an "I don't care" moment. Sometimes, he would dress like one. Hey, if you're comfortable with your body, you can do whatever you like. I was never one to judge. If I didn't like it, I just didn't get involved. He was a PC at Edinboro when I met him. As I asked around, he was one of the guys staying around for the summer, so it was a perfect fit for me. You didn't have to train somebody who worked at the school because they already knew what to do. He was a fun guy with a lot of ambition.

Never knew a lesbian at that time, so you get to learn a little bit about some people and the way they think. I hired a new girl to become my new personal care tenant. She told me she was a lesbian and then talked about her girl fights all the time. I was always like, "Why are you even dating a girl if you're gonna fight like this?" It was kind of funny. I'd always try to tell her ways to have a girl check her out, find interest in her, and bring her into her life. She was trying to be like a guy, so I knew that part. While working, she'd be on her phone looking to see if anyone had messaged her back for a date night or a night on the town. I'd always give my opinion on how I thought her babes looked. I'd say, "I like that one." We obviously didn't have the same taste because we always had a different choice. For the first time in my life, I shaved my head. I didn't have the right clippers, so it took us an hour to shave every hair off my head. Why? No idea, but it was probably just too hot. She worked for me for about a month and was a pretty cool girl, but too much drama.

It was hard for me to find a nighttime person because I always got home late at night from the races. That's when I found Faith in Earl. They lived in a trailer park, sleeping all day, getting up at 2:00 p.m., and then staying up all night. It was no problem for them to show up from twelve to two in the morning, sometimes bringing some of their fellow trailer parkers. And the funny thing? They never, ever shut the door. They'd be taking my clothes off, and then a person would be standing at the door talking to him like nothing was going on. One time, they brought a very attractive young lady. She was standing there watching while my pecker was hard. She said, "Boy, you have a very nice cock."

I replied, "Well, thank you." By this time, I didn't care if people saw me naked because it was just another day in paradise for me. One time, Faith brought a guy in who again stood at my open door. Faith and Earl picked up a used hot tub on the side of the road and then put it in their yard. While Faith was putting me to bed, John stood over by the door, asking Faith, "When are we gonna get in that hot tub so I can put this big ten-inch right up your ass?"

I had tears in my eyes, and then Faith replied, "Oh, just behave, will ya?"

One day, my brother and I were sitting near the bed. Earl brought his seven-foot-long iguana, threw it on my brother, and then he sent that reptile flying against the wall. He yelled, "Earl, get that fuckin' thing off me!"

Earl returned with "That thing doesn't bite. It's one of the nicest pets you could ever have."

Two days later, Faith came in with a bite in her foot that took twenty-seven stitches and then became infected by the saliva. I really got a chuckle out of that because my brother said, "I'm glad it wasn't me, or I would have killed it."

Faith and Earl were also swingers, and they often asked me to go with them. They always told me, "You could bang whoever you want. Nobody really cares, and it's a good time." I passed on that one. Those two were so much fun to work with. Don't even know what

really happened to them, but they always gave me a chuckle.

Pam was my racing girl. Her husband also raced cars at the local tracks, so she applied to my ad and then started working for me. We always had a lot to talk about, but 100 percent of the talks were racing. Sometimes, we would both race on the same track, while other times we race on different tracks. Weekends were always a replay of our racing events. She would go with me on trips to the racetrack, working as my personal care attendant, if we stayed the night. Her husband, Gary, would also come along to help us on the pit crew. I wish I could have had him full-time because that man was a lot of help. Guys that have their own cars are universal in the pits. You don't have to ask them to do something twice. They get it right the first time. One night, we went to a track that was two hours away. Matt raced the super late on Friday, but the motor overheated, so he pulled in. We spent the night working on the car all afternoon trying to correct the overheating problem. Matt couldn't race that night, so one of my heroes while young, Allen Dillenger, drove the super late that night, finishing fourth. On the ride home, I was having severe neck pains. Gary drove the trailer home while Pam rode with me. I had to stop at a rest stop to get a neck brace to put on my neck so it wouldn't droop down. Gary got home in about an hour and forty-five minutes, while Pam and I took about five hours. I think we got home at like four in the morning. She took it in total stride, but I felt bad that I put her through that. It was nice to see her at work and then again at the track later in the day. She was a lot of fun.

Then I had Dorcas. She was a gambler like myself. I liked to do scratch-offs once in a while, but I would never win anything big. She would always come in and show me her $2,000 winners, seeming like she won every time she scratched something off. I was like, "How much are you spending on this?" Because in my mind, you have to spend a lot, in order to win on those things. You just don't get lucky all the time. One time, she left me and then went down to the store, coming back twenty minutes later, showing me a $3,000 winner. She always told me that she only bought a few. I went down to the store, asking how long she was in the place and then how much she spent. They told me she could be there all morning. I'm going to play till I win. I'm a gambler, so I know the truth. We would go to the casino many times, always playing smaller bets. She would bet $0.40 one time and then $1.50 the next. I was like, "You can't win shit betting $0.40. You need to bet big to win big." Well, she bet the lowest amount and then got the five jacks on the screen. She won a hundred bucks and was very happy with that. I said, "If you had been betting bigger, you would have won $10,000." She was always a winner because gamblers always are. My gramma always said, "If you're a big winner, brag about it. If even, you had a great day. If a loser, tell them you ended up even." I still use this advice today.

Then I had Alberta. She worked at my favorite bar, Hunters Inn. Her husband was an avid hunter, so we talked about hunting too. She would tell me stories about how she would shoot a deer by putting the bow up in the air, just letting that arrow fly, and then the shot coming down, hitting the deer. She was so full of shit. I know how hard it is to hit one while aiming correctly at it. I'd laugh, and then she'd give me that bullshit smirk while walking away. I remember many times her getting stuck while driving in the snow to get me upright. My dad would have to go pick her up and then bring her to my house. Then they'd have to worry about getting their car back out so she could get home. I don't know how many times she did it, but it was a lot. I see her a lot at Hunters Inn, and then we still chat about days gone by. She was kind of like a grandma, just a nice lady.

I also had friends and neighbors. I grew up with Kristy, as she would always come over to play football with us when we were young. We never liked having a girl play with us, so she'd always get the hardest hits. If she wanted to play with us boys, she was going to

have to toughen up. As we grew older, we were kind of like best friends.

There was a time when I needed a PC, so I asked her if she wanted to work for me. She needed a job at that time, said yes, and then worked for many years, having great discussions every morning. I was always like, "Never thought you'd see me naked, huh?" Well, she saw the whole thing. I really didn't care. It had to happen. Much better than a brother or sister. You just never think a friend's going to get up and personal in your life, but it did. Kristy went with me to Challenger Speedway for a two-day show. On that occasion, many people came because my brother was asking Kelly to marry him. We stickered the side of the car with the question. The whole damn weekend rained out, so we had to unload the car so Kelly could read it. It would have been much better on the track, but we made it work. I remember Kristy getting very sick, sweating up a storm, but after a bathroom break, she was ready to go. Nothing like a good bowel movement. It was so convenient having a neighbor who could empty my leg bag, cook me lunch, or run over to help me anytime I had problems to be solved. Her girls were on call also, coming if anything was ever needed. She ended up working toward getting a teacher's degree and then got a job working in Maplewood. Kristy was a lot of fun in the morning, making my days go unwittingly quick.

Then I had my neighbor, Michelle. It was nice because she was also right next door, and if I ever needed anything, I could just give her a call or knock on the door. We would go out drinking a lot, and she helped me during long trips to the races. I would take the girl I was dating to her house and then drink until late in the night. Her husband was a Steelers fan, so we would always go back and forth on game day. Sometimes, the Steelers would beat my Seahawks, and then other times, my Seahawks would beat the Steelers. One time, they had a Fourth of July party, and we were lighting off fireworks.

We had tubes that shot the fireworks into the air after you dropped the boomer inside. We would stand the tubes straight up. We tried to do a double shot, putting two fireworks in at once. Well, after the fireworks went off, the second tube fell over and then aimed right at the whole crowd. I remember her husband running over, sliding on his stomach, tilting the tube up in the air just as it fired off. That was a close one because I was right in the line of fire. That same night, we were on the porch drinking some beers. There were four steps to get off the porch, so I impatiently got back a few feet and then floored it, jumping off their porch. It knocked the wind out of me, feeling like my whole spine collapsed. I'll tell you what, I'll never do that again. Drinking beer makes you do stupid things. Michelle was a good friend.

LeAndra was one of my nighttime girls. She was up to doing anything at any time. We went to many different places. We'd go to the casino, saving as much money as possible, to have a long day of playing. Hell, during my birthday, she brought me like $400 in scratch-offs. I was like, "You didn't have to do that," but she said, "I saved the money just for this occasion." What a sweetheart. And no, I did not become a millionaire. We got some of the money back but put it right back in and eventually ran out. I'm starting to hate scratch-offs more and more every time I play. Just no luck for me. Leandra also got to see my dad in his tighty-whities every night. My dad had a sugar fetish, so he would raid the cookie jar at about eleven thirty nightly, and then they would cross paths when she went to get me a snack. I'd always hear her chuckle when they made eye contact. Big Rich loves his cookies. We had Le'Andra go downstairs to the garage to get a pop. A gut-curling scream echoed through the house, sending her up the stairs, panting wildly, trying to catch her breath. We had my sister's Doberman in the garage locked up in the cage, barking at her. It looked like a heart attack waiting to happen. I found out real quick that she didn't like big dogs. Glad my girl was still alive, then settled down for a good laugh. She was a lot of fun too.

Next came longtime friend Denise. She was in my brother's grade and attending our same church. She always said that I didn't  talk to her much in school, but I felt like we had some different friends. Plus, I was a grade ahead of her, so I wouldn't have been in many of her classes. I saw her on the street one day, stating that if you ever need a personal care attendant, she'd like to do the job. About a year later, my morning girl was leaving, so I called Denise and offered her the job. She's been with me for over fourteen years, calling me her second husband. We do argue like we're married. We have been through thick and thin together. She came at four in the morning so I could go hunting and late at night after the races were done. We went gambling, went to see her favorite band, and ate at the finest wing bars. Her husband, Rob, always came up to gamble with me online, and he also cooked me his finest burgers. One day at the casino, we won a jackpot. I hit her in the back to congratulate each other, and the lady beside her said, "Did he hit you?"

She looked at her and then said, "Yeah, he beats me all the time."

You should have seen the look on that girl's face. You could tell that she always had a stick up her ass. I have been dropped a couple of times, but Denise only did it once. We had to call Rob to help pick me up and get me back in the chair. She always says it wasn't a hard fall. But I don't care. She dropped me. She's been there through my ups and downs, and she's always there when I need her. She would come to clean up shit or put me to bed after a long day, never complaining. Got to love that girl.

Lastly, I got Amy. My sister said a long-legged cute girl applied to my post. She was a cutie. She walked on the first day while I was lying there naked on the bed. Denise told her to get over here so she could see what needed to be done. Amy said she didn't know where to look, but if I saw a naked girl, I'd be looking. Amy has been working for me for about five years. Like Denise, she came at any point during the day when I needed help. If one of them went on vacation, the other one filled in for her. Both girls could do it morning or night. We had been to the races and casinos and went on dates two times a week. This girl knew my book for sure because she was the one who helped me do the outline for an hour or two every night. We would do a little bit each night, and then after writing each part, she would read it and then make sure it sounded okay. She is my night girl, always having a lot to talk about during those hours at night. I don't think either of us needs a lot of sleep. We would go to bed late, then always get up early in the morning. I am in a good spot right now with both of these girls, as they are there for me any time I need them. Hell, they even went to the hospital in Pittsburgh, spending the night many a time. Sure, it is nice to see a familiar face when you're in the hospital.

One funny story we had was during a date to Erie. We had just left a steak house and then headed home through Edinboro. While coming to the intersection, I hit the brakes, with nothing happening. I quickly swung into the gas station, through a stall, and then down over a bank toward the mall. As I came to rest, I looked at her and said, "What the fuck!"

The gas attendant had to think, "What the hell!" as I flew through there at about thirty-five miles per hour. Got lucky again, surviving another near-crushing blow. Amy has been my *rock* during these hard times, giving me happiness in my recovery years.

Then I got to include my sister Brenda. When I couldn't get a hold of those two girls, she was always the girl that took charge. She wasn't into cleaning shit, but she'd buckle down, then do it when it needed it done. She's like my dad; she's never easy on anything. Rolls me rough, getting the  job done, damn it. Brenda is awesome and always a straight shooter. When I get down at times, she tells me to get the hell off the sob story routine, get the hell over it, and then move on. She tells me, "I've seen you go through much worse things than this." No sugar-coating from her. Kick my ass, then I tie up my bootstraps, then start taking names. Well, I think you're cool, little sister. I always tell her, "You're my favorite sister," with her replying, "I'm your only sister."

Lastly, I got to include my mom and dad. They've been with me from the beginning, from the time in the hospital, all the way till now. They were my PCs for many years, including my brother and sister. They always did the best they could. Now I'd rather have my personal care attendance than have them work for me. They're getting older now, and it takes them a lot of time, looking like two bulls fighting in a ring. I don't have to say a word when my other girls are here, but I always have to comment when they're working on me. A few stories about my dad and mom were pretty funny. At least now, it's funny.

I was at a friend's wedding, and I brought this girl that I met at a bar. I didn't know her too well, but she was a very good-looking girl. We were at the wedding where I had about two or three beers while she had just drank one. After a while, it looked like she was absolutely hammered, and then she started rubbing me down and kissing me while sitting at the table. After a while, my dad's friend told me to take her home and put it to her. So I did. Took her home, at least. When I got home, she got into my bed and then passed out. Her skirt was up over her waist, exposing her panties. I could not get a blanket over the top of her, so I wondered what to do. I went to my neighbor's. She came to my rescue, putting the blanket over her. How crazy. When my mom got home, she told me to get her out of bed and take her home. I argued a bit and then just gave in and took her home.

The girl asked, "What's wrong with her?"

I replied, "That's just my mother."

Now what was really funny was a couple of nights later, she called it four thirty in the morning. Big Rich brought the phone down and then put it to my ear. Then she said, "I'm so horny. Could you talk dirty to me?" He was there standing in his tighty-whities, holding the phone, telling me to get talking. I told her my dad wanted me to hang up because it was four thirty in the morning. He hung up the phone, and then I never talked to that girl again. I think somebody slipped something into her drink because that girl was messed up after one beer. Got to love Big Rich.

Another time, I was in the shower with my mom. This was just after we built a new house, and we used the shower for about the third time. She leaned me forward to wash my back, and then I fell straight forward, smashing my face off the ground. I remember blood being everywhere and then the dog coming over to lick my face. I yelled, "Get that fuckin' dog out of here!" My mom just stood there, saying, "Oh god, oh god!" My sister came in and said, "Get him in the chair, get him off the ground!" They finally got me in my chair as I was cussing up a storm. My teeth went into my lip, swelling it up as big as a baseball. I sure as hell didn't want my mom doing a shower again. Thank God for my PCs.

CHANGING HOMES

After college, I lived at home for the next twenty years with Mom and Dad. My normal day started with an early five thirty in the morning wake-up. Get on the shitter, then take a shower. I'd be out the door into the school by about 7:00 a.m., then teach till about two thirty in the afternoon. Then head home to usually take a nap, wake up, and head to work on the race car or go hunting. I was busy, always having something to do. Even though I did sit all the time, I'd never sat around. My parents were getting up there in years, so I had to make a decision about moving in with my sister. She was building a new house, so I decided to move in with her when it was completed. My mom was looking out for me because she wanted to make sure that I had somebody to watch over me in my older years.

While they were building my sister's house, OVR came to see what equipment they could install to make my life easier. They helped with the cement in the front of the house where I'd be parking my truck. They also put a lift in the ceiling of my room so it could lift my fat ass in and out of bed without straining my girl's backs. That thing is pretty slick. You put a sling underneath me, lift me up in the air, and then slide me across so I can get in my chair. I used to jump into bed, then have the girls grab my legs, and put me in my chair. When I think about it now, it sure seemed like a real pain in the ass. I'm sure it didn't help their backs much, and it hurt me sometimes too. OVR also helped put in a shower. You could wheel right in that thing and then put the nozzle right at my level. I love the shower. It's my time of peace. I know my showers take a little long sometimes, but hell, I have to take it all in, getting myself prepared for the day.

I left home and then got a brand-new truck. I always had Ford vans, and then I went to a minivan. I was tired of being a soccer mom. Then while surfing the Internet, I found a place that converted trucks into handicapped vehicles. The owner of the business was actually a quadriplegic who designed all these. I thought it was the coolest thing I'd ever seen, so I decided to get one so I could load my own deer into the back. I was tired of everybody else just picking up my deer and then taking it to camp. I wanted to do it myself. The first thing I had to do was pick out my truck at the local dealer. Once we got the truck, we had to send it out to Illinois to a guy who designed the handicap part. It has a swinging door that kind of looks like a Lamborghini. It has a lift that comes out, then down. Once that was installed, it was sent down to Somerset, Pennsylvania, to get all the electronics put in it. They had it for about six months. The whole conversion took about one year to complete.

Then came the day of reckoning. I went down to drive my truck home. So we were three hours from home, and I was driving a vehicle that I'd never driven before. With all the conversions, the cost of the truck was about $175,000. I had to drive this truck home on the highway and was completely terrified. I had to pull off the road about six times during the ride home. Dad was always asking me, "What the hell's wrong with you?" I never had this problem in my other vehicles. There was just something missing, but we found it a couple of weeks later. I just needed a strap around my left shoulder to keep me from falling over. Every time I'd go around the corner, my body would shift to the right, and then I'd feel like I couldn't control the brake and gas. Just a $2 strap around my neck, and then I could drive that thing anywhere. Hell, the truck sat in my yard for about two weeks before I'd even get back in the thing.

Then my sister came over, saying, "Get your ass in that truck and start practicing." Once I put that strap on, I was a driving machine. I've stopped at stores before, and then the people come out wondering where I got this. I said for $150,000, you could get one of your own. OVR was definitely a blessing as I never could afford this on my own weekly paycheck, as they paid for all the conversions. I could get a new vehicle after either a hundred thousand miles or ten years, whichever came first. The only thing you had to have was a full-time job in order for them to help you. I can say this for sure: I finally feel like a real man. Got myself a truck, can load a deer in it, and put it in four-wheel drive to get out of any trouble. People are never afraid to approach me and then ask where I got the truck. They always say they've never seen anything like this before. I know at the time, there were two guys in Pennsylvania who had one of these trucks, so a lot of people would have never seen them before.

When I go to restaurants, I usually leave the side door open. It's just easier for me because then I don't have to open it up and put the lift back out when I get back in it. I don't know how many people come into the restaurant and then ask, "Sir, do you know your door is wide open?" I always come back with "If somebody can steal that thing, I'll shake their hand." There is a keypad that you must hit a sequence to get the thing started, so I'm not too worried about anybody taking anything. It's definitely a conversation starter. When Amy and I go out to eat, she always says, "You're going to leave this open? Somebody might steal the thing."

I said, "Hello, they won't." People are afraid of handicaps. They don't even come close because sometimes, we're like the plague. One thing's for sure, I love this damn truck.

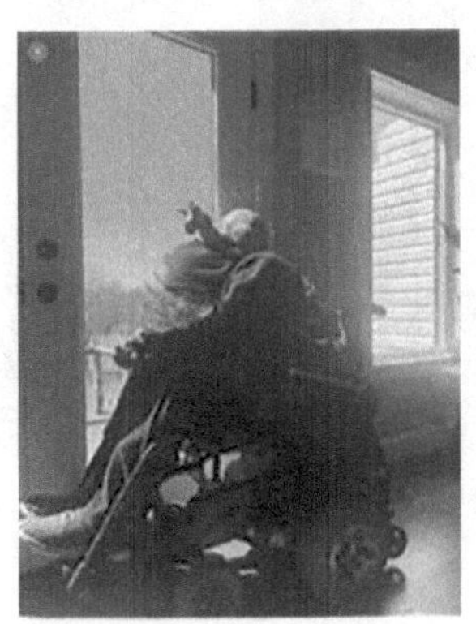

One thing about living at Brenda's is that she loves having pets around. Right now, they have three dogs and four cats. One of those cats is missing and hasn't been seen for about three weeks. I get along with just about all of them, but one of them really stands out as my best bud. That is Koba, a hairless cat. There also is his sister Kilo, who lives here too. Kilo is kind of a bitch, that just runs and hides, but Koba is totally the opposite. He'll crawl up on my shoes or my lap, then ride around with me on my chair. My sister got me a Dyson heater. While I lay in bed, he snuggled up beside me to get warmed up. If I go out in the living room to sit in the sun, Koba will jump right up on my head and then fall asleep there. Even when I'm eating, he'll crawl up on my lap, waiting for his portion. He always gives me an evil eye if I don't feed him anything. That cat is just loved by everybody in the family; it is definitely the favorite of the house. The one thing about Koba that you don't understand is that he never goes outside, regulated entirely to the house. These cats can get a sunburn if they go out when the sun hits their skin. If he ever gets stuck outside, he meows like crazy and then wants to get back in the house. Koba and I like the same things: food, heat, and women. We will always be together until one of us passes away because I'm always there for my buddy.

GETTING SICK

At the beginning of 2021, I sold my race car and trailer and was still teaching at the school. I wanted to teach until 2025 so I could pay off my vehicle and then relax for retirement. In February, my personal care attendant, Amy, wanted to learn how to change my catheter in case my mom wasn't around. This was normal. I usually did it once a month at that time, with Amy wanting to know how to do everything in my care. The problem? I usually lay flat when they insert a catheter, but this time, I was sitting against the wall while she was doing it. When she put the catheter in, I started seeing blood in my urine. I didn't know what the hell was going on, but they sent me to the hospital to check it out. After a while, the bleeding stopped, and then everything seemed to go back to normal, saying everything was okay. Within a few days, I was wheeling down the hall with my mom, telling me to drink more fluids. I drank three huge sixty-four ounces of jugs of water, then after an hour or two, my vision started to get blurred, and I could hardly sit up in my chair. I remember my mom asked, "Scott, what is wrong?" But I couldn't speak. Everything that came out of my mouth was blurry and un-understandable. She called the ambulance, and I was sent right to the hospital. They did some tests, finding out that I was septic. The catheter through my bladder wall must have caused some sort of infection that we didn't know about. Now I spent three weeks knowing nothing.

They ended up putting me in a coma that lasted for like three weeks. I was so messed up in the head because all my electrolytes were off, causing me to have crazy thoughts. While lying in bed, I thought I was a chicken because the bed looked so small. It looked like I had a human head, two little legs, and a breast for wings. I don't know why that was in my head, but boy, that's what I thought.

I remember asking the nurses, "Do I have chicken legs? Are they folding them down when you guys turn me?" It was a very crazy time for me, one that I've never experienced. After coming out of the coma, I remember my mother trying to get me in a chair so I could get used to it. When I sat, I would sweat so bad that I couldn't take it anymore, but she'd make me continue to sit there. I remember telling Dad that Mom was trying to kill me. They would give me some blue pill that I'd said, "It's a tranquilizer. She's trying to take me out, Dad."

He would always tell me, "Your mother's not trying to kill you."

I said, "Yes, she is." I always addressed her as the Wicked Witch at that time. Then I'd ask Dad if she had flown out on her broom yet. I even had certain nurses that I totally trusted, then others that I didn't care for at all, letting them know it. It's definitely something I only remember parts of, but they were totally crazy at the time. Here are some of my stories. So sit back and relax, and then take in this craziness.

After I came home from the hospital one time, my mom had a sixth sense, then felt like something was wrong with me. They came in a little earlier because they would flip me every two hours, finding out that I was unresponsive and that my lips had turned blue. I guess I had gagged on some phlegm, so I was not getting air to my lungs. They called an ambulance and then worked on getting a stronger pulse back into my body while heading to the hospital. I remember coming back to my senses while they wheeled me into the hospital. I had a respirator on that kept my lungs cleared so I could breathe freely, but I couldn't talk. In my mind, I was thinking that the nurses were going to give me a joint so I could relax. I remember trying to speak to my dad while he was in ICU with me. I couldn't write or speak at the same time, so I felt like I was helpless. I kept pointing to things, trying to tell my dad I wanted to have an alphabet so I could speak.

He would ask, "Do you want food? Are you hurting? Do you need a nurse?"

I kept shaking my head no to all those questions, and then when a male nurse finally showed up, I was pointing to different things on the wall.

He then stated, "You want an alphabet?"

I shook my head up and down, stating yes, and then they wrote the alphabet chart from A to Z.

I told my dad I could breathe, so have them take this tube out of my mouth. After a day of tests, the doctors finally removed the tube, and then I could speak again. I felt so helpless at that time, but I remembered, in my mind, that the whole table was filled with different kinds of weed, remembering the nurses telling me to try one so I could relax. I never relaxed with that thing in my mouth, and not one nurse really told me to smoke a joint. Just me being crazy again.

I don't know if folks remember those rat rod shirts that would always have those crazy-looking rats on hot rods riding around. You'd see him a lot on people who ride Harley-Davidson. My sister was staying with me one night. Then near midnight, she said it was time for her to leave. I thought I was in a bar where everything was totally upside down. The floor was on the ceiling, and then the ceiling was on the floor. I remember yelling to her, "Don't leave. There are three of them that are going to return very shortly, and I'm terrified. Don't leave me here." Of course, the best remedy to relieve craziness was more drugs, so they put you to sleep. The rats never did come, so I was happy about that because I probably would have jumped out of my skin. Boy, I would have liked some bar food at that time though.

Another time, Denise was with me, watching a horror movie. Or I think we were watching a horror movie. I remember looking to the corner of the room and seeing a space where a man was crawling through it. I remember Denise sitting on the bed, myself, and a guy wearing a scarecrow mask. He was sitting there, looking straight ahead, breathing heavily. I remember yelling to Denise, "Please don't go! You need to help me! Somebody's here to kill me!" I saw him coming from the corner of the room, and nobody stopped him. I sat there completely frozen by freight. I would hear him breathe deeply while I was holding my breath. I really don't remember how it ended, but Denise repeatedly said there was nothing there. What the hell's wrong with me?

Then another crazy moment. I remember riding in the back of an ambulance with Mom and Amy as they were dressed in these hospital gowns, looking like nurses. For some reason, I thought my blood pressure cuff was a shocker. If I did or said anything negative, they would shock me. I would always tell people the next day that Amy and Mom were trying to kill me. They were shocking me all the time, so I was losing it in my mind. All I could smell was glue that held reflection stickers on their uniforms. Every time that cuff would blow up for my blood pressure, I thought I was getting shocked, yelling for somebody. The Wicked Witch and Black Widow were at it again, trying to take me out, regulating them to the bottom of my list of people I wanted to see. In my mind, I really couldn't trust anybody at that point.

Before I got hurt, a guy with Raven bows was going to make a video of me shooting a buck. When COVID-19 hit, all that went away, and I didn't have a chance to make a video with him. While in the hospital, I did make a video. I remember a six-point walking out, then waiting for a good shot so I didn't screw up the video. We have to promote a good bow for these people, so make this shot a good one, and don't screw it up. I was under so much pressure, so I waited for the perfect shot. For the first time hunting with a film crew, I wasn't afraid to pull the trigger and then shoot that buck. There I was, sitting with the Raven crew, with the cameras rolling. In my mind, I was trying to come up with a big speech that sounded knowledgeable about deer hunting. And, of course, the art of the hunt and shot placement. Thank God for allowing us to harvest such a majestic creature. I had it all just about summed up, like a pro. I remember telling people as they came in that I made a hunting video, then they could watch it.

They'd ask, "Well, where is it at?"

I said, "I don't know. They were here a few hours ago and said it would broadcast in a few weeks." I guess I should have asked them where it would be. Dad jacked me quite a bit about the story, but I came back with crazy answers continuously. All I can say is more drugs, more drugs.

Another time, when I was alone, I gazed at the ceiling, seeing spiderwebs threaded all over my room. I remember hearing a whispering voice telling me, "If the creature's little stinger pricks you,

you'll die instantly." This killer looked like a praying mantis and would constantly climb down the web toward me. I filled the room with fearful screams, waiting to die. A lot of things come to your mind when it's your last time on earth, terrifying me to the fullest. Thankfully, a nurse came in and then asked what I was screaming about. I told her, "Thank God you saved me. I was about ready to get bitten by that evil entity." It was within inches, but I was crazy, crazy, I was.

One time, I opened up my eyes, thinking I was in a barn. A bunch of my friends were sitting around in lazy boy chairs smoking stogies. I also remember two little dragons sitting on the ledge, saying, "Yeah, yeah, he's right. He's right." They were both smoking little stogies also. I looked out through the window and then saw guys playing Jarts. They were throwing them high up in the air while other people were running around trying to avoid them. Like, where did that come from? We were talking about hunting, then chasing women. I remember thinking, *Well, I have a few hot nurses. Maybe they'll come in, and we can check them out.* I don't know why we were in a barn filled with hay bales, horses, and stalls. I was not accustomed to hanging out there, so why did it pop into my head? I have no idea. I'd close my eyes and then feel like I'd slept three or four hours, only to open them and see that only one minute had gone by. Those were some long nights.

One afternoon, when my dad came in, I told him I'd won the lottery. I kept hearing those sounds of triple dings running through my head. *Ding, ding, ding.* It sounded just like a slot machine going off after a big win. In my mind, I saw the three triples hit on the TV screen worth $2.4 million. I told my dad about it, and then he said, "Scott, you didn't win anything." I kept stressing and checking my account. There was going to be $2.4 million in it by the end of the day. A few days later, my dad came back and then told me that there was nothing like that in the account, just what I get each week for my school payment. I kept saying that was bullshit. I was a big winner, and they were going to put it in there. "You need to call somebody and then find out where my money's at."

My dad said I was hell-bent on getting that money, even though I probably never came close to winning anything like that. My mind was a very crazy winner during that moment.

Then I told my mother we were staying in Flintstone huts. They were rock buildings with little fires set in the middle of them. They all had holes in the roofs, with smoke billowing out from the inside. I remember one of the guests carrying around a tetradactyl leg and then throwing it on the fire. I wasn't eating a lot at that time, so my lips were wet and ready to dig into that baby. All these huts were built into a side hill, with a path that took them down to each level. The first day I got there, I wheeled around until I found a hut that said "Bidwell" on it. All the people were very generous, even handing me a pair of deerskin shorts to wear. They even had dots on them like the Flintstones had. Why was I thinking of that? I have no clue because I haven't watched *Flintstones* in like forty years. My electrolytes being out of WAK made me hallucinate, the doctor said.

Another time, I woke up from a deep sleep and then kept hearing the words, "Cocaine, cocaine, you're on cocaine." To me, it was coming from the IV drip that was going into my arm. I was telling my dad, "Go get the nurse, and then get this cocaine out of me. They're going to arrest me."

He kept asking me, "What the hell were you talking about?"

I said, "Listen, the IV box is saying, 'Cocaine, you're on cocaine.' I've never been a criminal my entire life, so at that point right there, your heart goes to the center of your throat." I was waiting for people from the police to come in any second and then arrest me. Then I remember a movie Tom Cruise was in, where he played a drug dealer who flew drugs on a plane. I think I watched it a couple of weeks before that, so the sound of the word cocaine made me think of that movie. Boy, everything felt like it was real. How much more can I take?

One time, I woke up from another deep sleep and heard a humming sound coming from my bed. It wasn't my bed, but it was coming from my head. I looked at the wall that was completely white, thinking I was in heaven. I remember physical therapist Melvin walking in and then asking me how I was doing. I remember asking him if he was my preacher giving me my last rights. He chuckled about it and then told me he wasn't. My dad again was like, "What are you talking about? You just woke up. You're in a hospital bed." There were so many times that I really didn't know what was going on, but in my head, I was actually terrified. How do you protect yourself when you're terrified like that? My dad finally calmed me down and then told me I was still here on earth. Need more drugs in my drip? Let's move on. I kept thinking it was drugs they were giving me, but I later learned it was an electrolyte imbalance.

This is funny, at least in my mind. I remember seeing somebody wearing a shirt that had Bidwell on the back, with checkered flags across it. I remember it saying he had a hundred feature wins and was a multitime track champion. I was all excited at that point because I didn't remember Dad racing anything in my lifetime.

I asked Mom, "When did Dad race? While growing up, I didn't remember him ever being behind the wheel."

She laughed and then said, "Your dad never raced anything but a mower. Why are you thinking this stuff up?"

"I saw somebody wearing a shirt with Bidwell on it who said he had a hundred wins."

I remember Amy playing a song that night that had Bidwell running to the front as the chorus. At least, that was what I thought they were saying. I'd want her to play that song over and over. I was so proud of my dad, how well he did, and how I must have been so successful in my racing career. That was funny because we bought my dad a driver's experience package to drive a race car at Tri-City Speedway for one year. They gave him twenty minutes to hot lap a dirt-modified race car. I can tell you this: he never got up to speed. I remember my uncle running along the fence as my dad was coming out of the corner, ending in a virtual tie at the flag stand. That is bad. Nope, my dream was not true. The flagman ripped his arm out of the socket, trying to get him up to speed, but my dad just putted around. He thought he was flying, telling me, "I don't know how those guys get around there with twenty-four cars out there." Fun times in my mind.

Lastly, my vision was so messed up that when somebody would walk into my room, I'd close my eyes and then open them to see them beside my bed, holding my hand. They'd ask me how it was doing, hoping things were going well. I remember asking, "Why is my vision so fucked up?" I opened my eyes, you're here, close them, then open them to see you way over there. I guess it had something to do with my kidneys. The drugs I took put so much strain on my kidneys that my vision had me going crazy. I remember watching an NFL football game one night, and the guys looked like they were in slow motion at one point. Then there'd be a play the very next moment where they're standing in the end zone. They still had eighty yards to go. What did I miss? The entire drive? I watch movies on Netflix right now. I remember parts of it but never the entirety of the story. That scared me more than anything. Could you imagine a blind handicap? Can't feel, can't see, won't see much more of me. That rhymed pretty well. It wouldn't be much to live for, but everything eventually came back to normal. Thank you, God.

HOSPITAL STAYS

WHEN THEY FIRST moved me to the hospital, I was moved to the intensive care unit, and that was when COVID-19 started. I don't remember seeing the nurses very often, as I'd always have to call to get their attention. Well, I might not be with it enough to even call them. That's when I got my first sore on my rear end. I don't believe I was turned enough, getting sores on my tailbone. After about three weeks in the hospital, then another week to recover a bit more, I was sent home. I was still all screwed up and had a PICC line in my arm that allowed me to put the drugs in my line when infections occurred so we didn't have to go to the hospital. I remember my mom trying to set me up every night, and then I would sweat very badly. In the past, when I sweated, there was something wrong, or I sat too long. Of course, that didn't enter my mind at that time because I was still so messed up. Then one night, after my personal care attendant threw me in bed, Amy saw blood on the sheets. She rolled me over and then saw five sores, three on my back then two on my backside. I was sweating but couldn't feel them, so I didn't know at the time this was happening. If my mind was right, I would have known that something was wrong and then laid back in bed. What this did was put me in a three-year battle for my life, thus taking away my freedom.

I went to the wound clinic once a month so they could check my sores and then clean them out in case they were infected. It was the start of a long, painstaking ordeal, but three of them healed pretty quickly. They put a wound vac on my back so it would suck all the excess drainage out of the wound. When I first started, I had five wounds on my body, many taking an hour to two hours for them to put on while I was lying on my side. You think I hated life? You're damn right, I did. While the wound vac was on, I couldn't take showers but two times a week on Tuesday and Friday. Those were the days that the nurses came to put on a new set of wound vac pads. The wound vac is like a suction in which excess fluids are removed, like a vacuum cleaner. This unit runs continuously all day long and all night. When the airtight seal comes off, the vac starts beeping very loudly. *Beep, beep, beep.* Sometimes, they'd come off at two or three in the morning, and then my mom would have to call their hotline to ask for help. I would always yell, just rip them off, then put a wet-to-dry patch on them. Damn it, I didn't want to lay here all night. Sometimes, it took a hell of a lot of time for her to actually fix the leak instead of just ripping them off like I wanted to. It seemed like I never had a say in anything, but I made it a point later down the road.

My sister and mom were trying to get me up more so I could go outside. I decided to go outside one day, placing my ass in my old chair, heading to the pond. I was not going to be up very long, so they didn't put pants on me, just a blanket to cover me up. On this day, they did not strap my feet onto the footrest, so I might have problems if I leaned forward too much. While driving down, my mother told me to slow down because I hadn't gotten up for a long time. I told her, "I got it. This is no big deal. I can drive this thing." As I got closer to the pond, I put the brakes on and then fell forward on top of my joystick. The chair started going around in circles, getting closer to the pond each lap. Just then, my sister ran over, pulling me off the joystick.

She asked, "Why didn't you scream?"

I replied, "I was holding my breath because I felt like I was going to be driving into the pond." Nobody else in my family ran toward me or tried to save me. Thank God Brenda was there. Dad had his one-liner, of course.

He said, "All I saw was butts and nuts." Since I didn't have pants, I was buck naked under there, showing my family jewels. Lucky to live again.

Yes, a lot of my friends came in to see me, but that's not how I liked them to see me. Yeah, it feels good, but at that point, I was pretty lost. Again, I thought about what kind of life I was going to have. Have I said that before? One time we went to Pittsburgh, and then I asked the specialist about my ass. He was brutally honest, telling me it might take five to ten years to heal my wounds. I had a big lump in my throat, and then at that point, I was like, why do I even want to be here? Flipping to my side for hours, taking two showers a week, and lying in bed constantly for hours upon hours every day. I saw every Netflix movie that they offered, then repeated it for every daytime show. The only good thing was the PICC line in my arm, so they could draw blood right from the tap. Thank God I didn't have to get poked because, in the hospital, they were in there every two hours, draining blood from me. No wonder I had to get blood transfusions, getting about five of those. My wound did bleed a bit, but these people were damn vampires. I always liked them to draw it from my hand because I couldn't feel it. I was like, if I can't feel my hands, there's no way in hell that they're going to drain it from any other spot I could feel.

They would say, "You're running out of veins."

Then I'd say, "I don't care. Find one."

They always prevailed. At one point, it took seven times to draw my blood. How do you like that, folks? I'm used to needles by now, but it doesn't mean I like them. Now on to my VNA girls.

I got VNA nurses every Tuesday and Friday morning. I saw all kinds of personalities, always laughing at my stupid jokes. Even though this was exhausting for me, I usually made them laugh. I mean, what else did I have to do? I like making people laugh. I had good days and bad, but I sure hated that wound vac. That involved almost two hours on my side every single Tuesday and Friday. We talked about everything, including a lot of stories in this book.

I said, "You're going to laugh when you hear some of this stuff and not going to believe it's true." I told them some folks thought I shouldn't say a lot of the things that are in this book, but I'm telling you, this is about me, what I had to worry about, and the many fears I dealt with each day. I had a lot running through my mind, worrying about how I should tell people about how a handicapped person lives their life. I lived a great life, but it was not all flowers and roses,

I can tell you that. There were fun times, then outrageous times, that I wanted to tell everybody. The nurses were my test run, with them stating, "You'll put a smile on their face." So I put everything in this book that happened to me because inquiring minds want to know.

During downtime alone, I really thought a lot of bad thoughts. How could I do myself in? I cried many nights, wondering what my life was going to be now. I was like, I have the mind now, but I don't even have the body. I was on the go all the time, never letting anything get in my way. It was go, go, go. This puts you in your place, you think a lot, and they're not all good. I was trying to figure out ways to do myself in because my wounds were getting infected all the time. I was still getting the wound vac all the time, then lay there for many hours. In my mind, I was like, *Why am I doing this? This is what I'm going to do all my life because I really don't want to be here.* The medical center told me there was nothing they could do. At that point, I'd really had enough. I told everybody, "I'm just going to live this out until I die because I don't want to do this anymore." Unbelievably, I was giving up. Mom and Dad agreed with what I said and then prepared to get me to that point. Mom really didn't want to give up, but she was granting my wish.

Amy, my nighttime care attendant, sat with me one night. She grabbed my hand and then started to cry. She pled, "You can't die. You need to be here and fight this. I really need you, and I'm going to be so lonely if you leave." Amy was very special to me, as she took me on dates every Tuesday and Thursday. We talked about everything at night, including what was going on in our lives. You could quiz me, and then I'd tell you everything about that girl. She told me many times, "You're my everything." I don't know what those tears did, but I wanted to live. I went into the hospital a couple of days later, and they then told me that I either had to go to Pittsburgh or I wasn't going to be saved. It was late at night, and then I made a decision to head to Pittsburgh. I was going to try one more time.

We left about one in the morning from Meadville, heading down to Pittsburgh. That ambulance was flying because it took us about an hour and twenty minutes to get to Allegheny Hospital. We got to the room at about 3:00 a.m., and a whole collage of people gathered in my room. They were all specialists in one area or another, asking me questions about every aspect of my situation, from medications to catheters, going to the bathroom, my injury, and anything to do with my care. They had a very good staff down there, taking very good care of me. The only problem? They were dragging their feet constantly. People would come in in the morning and then say they were doing this or that. Later at night, they'd say they were going to do this procedure, then do nothing. I was there for about nineteen days, but it took up to fourteen days before they finally decided to have surgery on my hip. That's what we talked about and the reason I went down.

I remember one doctor saying, "Well, you're going to be sent home tomorrow."

My mom got down on the floor and then said, "Over my dead body, you will not move him out of here until you give him surgery on his hip."

Well, a day later, I was going into surgery. They drilled about a silver dollar-sized hole in my hip that went in about twelve centimeters. You could drive a truck in that damn thing. They talked about sweating, then some bleeding, and I did that. While I was down there, my parents were there most days, with my girls coming down on Tuesday and Thursday to stay with me. I love my girls. We just sat there and then talked about what was going on at home, trying to keep me upbeat. If I ever needed anything, those two were there for me at every single turn. Believe it or not, it's nice to get away from my mom and dad too. I was there a few more days, and then to my surprise, they sent me home. Home is where I get the best care, so I got my pills on time, then got to sleep in my own bed, watching any channel I wanted. I got to take showers every day and didn't have that fuckin' wound vac anymore. I remember when Denise washed me, about ten pounds of dirt came off me. They tried to give me bed beds in the hospital. I didn't want them because I didn't want to move much, so the dirt was caked on me. It felt so nice to be cleaned up, finally home, and doing what I wanted to do, which was still looking at the ceiling.

One night, when I was in Pittsburgh, just doing nothing, Denise was staying with me till my parents came in the morning. We were farting around, looking for things to do, when she came up  with the different memes of one of the pictures we took together. We had about fifteen different memes at the time, but I selected this one for the book. I'm not going to be a tranny anytime soon, but I'll tell you what, I look pretty damn good as a woman. I didn't know if I'd ever look this good as a girl, but I was one hot bitch. I sure wouldn't want to hang on with my friends looking like that, or they'd have been all over me. Just little things like this always helped me get through the insanity of being in the hospital too long. Thanks, Denise, for the memories. It was a lot of fun.

Well, now I kind of had a new look on life. I went seven months without having any antibiotics put in my pick line. The hole in my ass, that was a silver dollar size, now had shrunk down to mere millimeters. The only thing I still have? Four inches of tunnel in my rear that I have to fill each day with packing. I now only take about ten minutes to do my wounds, which is a big improvement from two hours. The wound on my left hip is now almost flat on my ass and nonexistent. I asked the doctor the other day if he thought the tunnel would ever heal, and he said he used to be able to move his Q-tip up in there from side to side quite a bit, but now it's tightening up. He said, "Yes, they could close up." It's going to take more time, but I'm glad I made this choice. I have all the time in the world, but I still don't like lying in bed that much. When I get up, I still sweat a bit, sometimes feeling best when I'm in bed. I need to have days in bed, but nothing like before.

At this point, I had my PICC line removed, so I no longer had that in my arm. My sores are healing, so I'm sitting up from ten to thirteen hours a day. The only problem I have now is I'm bored. When I got sick, I retired from teaching, sold all my racing stuff, and couldn't hang with my friends all the time because they were still working. I used to always be on the go, doing something with my time. Now with my time, I don't do much but sit in the sun and watch TV. When I'm up, I still like to play on the computer for a few hours. This book has saved me in a lot of instances because it keeps my mind fresh, thinking of past things I've done. It's also keeping me busy, which is how I live my life daily.

If you want to lose weight, head to the hospital, but make sure you have good insurance to pay for it all. At the time I went into the hospital, I weighed 208 pounds, and then after about three or four times in the hospital, I was 158 pounds. How's that for a good diet? I bet if a person was selling salt in the hallway, people would pay an arm and a leg to get it. There are no spices at all in a hospital. Everything seems to be as dry as a popcorn fart. Never just take what they give you. You can always ask for whatever you like. There is a secret menu, where you could order a hamburger, toasted cheese, mac and cheese, or even pizza on the secret menu. They all at least looked pretty good, with some food tasting pretty good too. Occasionally, Denise or Amy would bring in some treats that I could eat undercover. Mom would bring me Arby's sandwich or occasionally bring me a pizza of my favorite brand. I always liked Menino's Pizza, which is the best in town for me. When I was in Pittsburgh, I got Papa John's because they don't have it around here, except for Erie. So I did get some good pizza at times, but all I can say is, bring your spices because they have none.

When I was in the hospital, I was pretty dirty at times. Some of it was my fault, as I didn't want to get washed because moving around really hurt my body. Due to my wounds, I could only lay on one side for a short period of time, and then I'd have to lay flat. Any kind of movement would make me sweat. Of course, that would make me dirtier. Another thing that really bothered me in there was doing my bowel movements. At home, I sat on a chair that wheeled over the toilet. If they had a chair, Denise would come in and help me out. If they didn't, I just had to shit in the bed. I don't know how that makes anybody else feel, but it drives me nuts. How those nurses deal with that every single day just really puts things into perspective. One night, my dad was standing by the door, and then one of the nurses rolled me, and I let out a fart that would blow down your house. Those girls never stopped working or even fazed them. Dad just laughed, patting them on the back from a distance because he was glad they were handling the situation better than he ever could.

Like I said, I love my showers. It's so nice to get one every day, like I do now. You just feel clean, where sweat is nonexistent. Did you ever use one of those non-rinsing shower caps placed on your head at the hospital? They say, "Oh, they're so good, and you'll really like it." To me, it's like putting chalk in your head, where you're itchier than you were before you tried cleaning it. So I passed on that cap, just sticking with what I had, a dirty old head. For me, it's very disappointing that hospitals don't have at least one wheel in shower because we are dirty people too.

People did take great care of me, as I made it through everything with flying colors. At one point, it was touch and go for me, but I had people on my side to help pull me through my deposition. I must thank Dr. Williams because he's always been at my side. My mother and personal care attendants have him on speed dial for any questions they might have about me. He always takes the time to thoughtfully answer any question or suggestion we may have. He is a great man, so I hope his Cleveland Browns win big someday. That man is a die-hard, so I'm wishing his boys the best of luck and a Super Bowl win within these next couple of years.

They had a couple of blunders in and out of the hospital. One day, I was heading into the wound clinic to get my sores looked at. We went through the normal procedure of checking them out, recording the depths, and then packing them again before I left. I'm always excited to see the ambulance guys arrive because I know it's time for me to get home. The guys were moving me from the bed to the stretcher, pulling me on a draw sheet. One of the EMTs pulled the stretcher back so the other guy could come around to get on the other side. I could feel my body start to float in the air as I started to fall to the ground. One of the EMTs grabbed my arm, which actually kept me from hitting the ground hard but pulled all the muscles in my shoulder. How do you like that? Hurting yourself in the hospital? By an ambulance crew to boot. It had taken about two weeks for the muscles to finally get some strength in them and the pain to go away. To this day, I still have some shoulder pain, but I sure hope that goes away.

This one's very funny but disgusting at the same time. Just before bed, my stomach had been rumbling loudly, making continuous sounds of a big blowout. Amy got me turned into position, and then I fell asleep until late in the night. At about three in the morning, I could smell something through my CPAP mask. At that point, I think I crapped the bed, but I didn't know for sure. I put my hand under the covers and then fluffed them a little bit to see if the smell would come to my face. My sister came in and then turned off my heat because I was getting too hot. She walked to the kitchen to get a glass of water, and then I pulled the mask back up on my face. I could feel wetness all over my face and mask, but I still didn't really know what had happened at the time. Then I got a sour taste of feces in my mouth and yelled to my sister to come back. I told her, "I think I crapped and then put it all over my face in my face and mask." She came into the room, turned on the lights, and then saw crap all over my face, lips, and CPAP. She was like, "Oh my god, you got shit everywhere." It took her about an hour, but she finally got me cleaned up. She put my hand in a tub of water and then washed my CPAP mask until all the shit had disappeared. The mask still stunk for about two days until we got it cleaned up in vinegar. To tell you the truth, I couldn't sleep very well those next two nights because of the smell. From now on, if I think I did go, I'm keeping my hand above the sheets. Boy, did that suck.

SCOTT BIDWELL FIELD DEDICATION

DENISE WAS A good friend in high school but turned out to be a better friend after taking care of me. She went to the school board, asking them about cleaning up the field house and then having it dedicated to me. Once the dedication was finalized, that girl was a go-getter. She would come up to the field house daily, getting paint all over her pants, face, and shirt. At that point, I couldn't really get out much, so I didn't see how they were proceeding with the field, but they would always inform me that things were going well. Some of my family members would show up to help her and her husband work in the field. They painted the press box, bleachers on both sides, field house, and even the field the night of the game. Everything looked immaculate, even the big sign on the field house created by my last driver, Brandon Groters from Phantom Graphics. Then he also printed shirts, sweatshirts, and hats with dedication symbols printed on them. Brandon also printed stickers for people with my number on it. I see people still wearing memorabilia from that event today.

For me, it was a total honor. I was just an ordinary kid trying to play the game I loved. I don't think of myself as anybody special, just an ordinary guy, wanting to play sports, hunt, and fish with my friends. I just wanted to hold down a job, make my parents proud, make life worthwhile, and have fun. Like Amy always tells me, "You're so hard-nosed. It's not even funny." I'm glad I was that way because I never would have been able to conquer the situation put forth in front of me. I worked hard to get what I have and then helped many people who might not have had the opportunities I did. I know a couple of times I'd look on the Internet to see what would come up if you typed your name in a search engine. When I put my name in there, I see Facebook pictures, stories, and places I've been. I see stories about the golden apple that I got in school. All this was done with people helping me and then me helping them. Even though I was in a chair, I never felt like I was. People never treated me like I was either. I was just a guy who loved life and the people that I shared it with. Just seeing the people who came out to support my life really made me feel good inside.

Denise's husband, Rob, took me up to the school in a minivan donated by Palmiero Toyota of Meadville. He drove me in front of the grandstands before the game had started. As I got out, the stands were full, with everyone cheering for me. I saw fellow teachers, former students, my family, and most of the friends I grew up with. I took a few bows and then wheeled toward the sign mounted on the field house. I had kids running beside me, in front of me, and around me. It was quite a sight to see. I felt like the Pied Piper leading all the kids to the sign. The sign was covered up, and then, after a few minutes, they unveiled it. Brandon did a hell of a job because it stands out even from the road. Then I got on the microphone, thanking everybody for coming and everyone who donated for the beautiful unveiling. Mostly, Denise for making my special day look outstanding. It's the best the place has looked, even when it was brand new. For me, it was pretty chilly outside, so I wheeled back to the van with Rob, and then we sat off to one side, watching the game. People were coming up to the van and then talking to me while I sat inside with the heat blowing on me. It was nice to finally get out because I had been bedridden for almost two years to that point. Realistically, I didn't even know if I was going to be able to make it, but I had to. By halftime, we loaded up and then headed home. I got put back into the bed that I'd been spending so many hours in and then smiled about my day. Denise, you did one hell of a job, and the community did great in helping make it a special day for me.

And what about the people on Facebook? Denise set up a GoFundMe page to help raise money for the event. In all, Denise raised about $19,000 from the community. All that went to paint, signs, shirts, sweatshirts, weight room, and decorations for the field. What can you say about people? After Denise posted the ad, it didn't take very long to get to that amount. I remember the days when they helped build our house. This felt the same way because the community always comes together to help one of their own. All I know is when I'm dead and gone, my legacy will not have been forgotten. I'm kind of here forever. Thank you, Denise and community.

The Latta brothers also brought their race car up to the school. The decal package depicted the color of the Saegertown Panthers, their logo, and my football #27 on it, with the name Beef inside the number. The front of the car also had my senior picture wearing my 27 jersey on it. The car looked beautiful. It was so unbelievably cool to have those guys take the time to put that on their car for my special day. That's the way their family was; they were always around when there was a special day or family event, which always included me. Yes, they brought racing into my high school dedication. My time with them meant so much to me, so sharing their love of racing with my love of football brought a fitting end to my day. A big thanks to my friends and family, the Lattas.

My goals. First of all, I want to get over these sores. I have one sore left, with a tunnel of about four inches deep, then about the width of a Q-tip. I've sat in bed many at times, thinking about which is worse, breaking my neck or having these sores. I was back to normal in about seven months after my neck injury, but now going on three years with these sores on my ass. They both have their drawbacks for sure, but the one on my ass is just ongoing. If I sit up straight for too long, I start to sweat because of my wounds. Then I tip back, taking pressure off my backside, which helps decrease my sweating. The sweating really is my biggest pet peeve. If it is colder, really breezy, or wet, that drives me nuts. I just can't seem to get my body temperature up, and then I always feel like I'm freezing. So sometimes, being back in bed is just relaxation for me. Amy always tells me it's better than I was a year ago, and it's going to get better from here on out. She's always so positive. I don't have that same feeling. This would be tough on anybody, as I tell her, name some names that could make it in this situation. It really does take a special person to be able to have this done to you or your life, especially when you are so independent. Like I said before, having your mind's ability to think and not being able to do anything can really drive a person insane. Thank God for my family and friends.

Next, I want to say goodbye to my nurses. Yes, girls, I loved you. You always came in with a positive smile and then tried to keep me upbeat. I was either funny or stupid, but you always laughed at me. I'm sure it's a very hard job to do, then go places that you really don't want to go to. I was told by Tiffany that I'm the place she loves to go the most. Tiffany gives it right back to me like I give it to her. I know one thing: she's so very loud, getting her point across like a loud crow or foghorn. They all did a great job keeping me as healthy as I could be during this downtime in life. At the present time, I am now down to seeing a nurse one time a week. They would usually come on Tuesdays and Fridays, with therapy coming on Mondays and Wednesdays. Slowly but surely, I went down to one day with the nurses, and now I don't need a therapist anymore. They still have to test my blood every week because all the antibiotics may have damaged my kidneys a bit, so I must keep an eye on them. Well, I thank all of them for helping me through this. And yes, we have improved quite a bit since that first day with five sores. I love you, ladies, but get the hell out. I'm ready to rock again.

What do I really want? I want my independence back. I want to be able to get up without worrying about wounds and then just go. I just want to have something to do instead of being bored. Like I said before, teaching keeps you young, and I want to be in that atmosphere. I can see where the elderly get older and then lose a lot of their friends, hitting the loneliest part of their life. I don't want to be part of that because I love being around people we make each other go. I need to get control of the sweating wounds, heal them, and have a healthy rear. Some people tell me to turn down the heat so that I won't sweat as much, but I always tell them that it has nothing to do with it. I could sit in my truck with ninety-nine-degree heat, then not sweat a bit. I use that heat to dry me off more than anything else. Right now, if I go out, Amy brings a separate shirt. After I sweat a bit, she changes to a fresh shirt. Once I tilt back and then rest a bit, the day goes on pretty much as normal. It also helps to be about seventy-five degrees or better, then the sweat tends to evaporate, and my shirt doesn't feel as wet. If I can get all those problems handled, I might get back to being the person I was before. I need to get to more races and sporting events then hanging out more with my friends and family without feeling miserable. I just can't believe how independent I was after I broke my neck, but these wounds have just totally drowned me. But I'm keeping my chin up until the end because we are only here once.

HOW DO I WANT TO LIVE?

WHAT'S A NORMAL life for me? I want to be able to get up at six thirty or seven in the morning and get back to working or subbing at school. I want to get back to a garage, help a local race team, and give them some pointers. Then I go to bed around eleven or twelve at night because I need about six hours of sleep a night. What's really funny is I used to sit on my ass for about eighteen hours a day without doing a weight shift. Now I have to do them every ten to fifteen minutes. I thought my thick Polish ass would always keep me upright, but it gave out when I became septic. I want to just get up and go, not have to plan my day ahead of time. I want to help the boys' basketball team fine-tune their skills, so they play at the highest level. I want to be able to hunt all six weeks again, hang out at camp, and chat with all the boys about deer stories like before. Really, just live without any restriction and get full independence back. I still have a world to see, and there is a dirt late-model race at Eldora. I'm ready to live again and be me. I'm not one for giving up.

While writing this book, I tried to think of a great title to put an exclamation point on my life. At the time, I thought about it being *Eight and a Half Lives*, but I surpassed that a long time ago and should have been dead by now. After I posted about writing a book, I saw one of my former Saegertown alumni, Rob, call it *Full Throttle*. That word stuck with me throughout the writing of this book, and I decided that's what my life was all about. That's the direction I wanted to go, telling the whole story about my life in the fast lane. I was never one to sit around as this book has stated, "Just go, go, go." So *Full Throttle* was the title I was going to go with because it's me.

As I finished this book, I looked back to the time lying on the table, waiting for anything to move. I was frightened, thinking I'd lost my chance at having a normal life. From that point on, I never once complained about my life. These were the cards that were dealt, so I damn sure picked them up, then played my hand. Through hard work, I did every single thing I wanted to do in life. I remember a kid telling me in rehab that there were 999 things we could do out of 1,000. The only thing we couldn't do was walk. If there was something I wanted to do, we rigged it up so I could do it. If there was something I needed, we made it. There was no end to what we could do. You can always adapt and make your life exciting and memorable. Even as I was writing this book, I looked back, then thought, *Look at all the shit I did*. I laugh about what my dad always asks, "Do you know what you could have if you didn't do all that racing and gambling?" I surely had time to think about it when I lay in bed, let my mind race, searching for a response. I would have made all that money, got septic, had all these sores, and then laid in a bed, doing nothing my whole life. How many people work all their lives, get all set up for retirement, then pass away? That was not going to happen to me. I was going to live life in the fast lane and then pass away because I wore my body out. Money is not everything, but it allows you to have fun. I'm so glad I had fun at an early age and then continued it every day of my life. All I can say is thank you. I can't even begin to describe how many people have made statements about my life. Many helped me get through fear, exciting times, and hard times, but every time, we overcame and grew. When people ask me about how my life was in a chair, I always respond, "I had a great life." I've done more in this wheelchair than most people do on a walking day.

To end this, I describe my life as a big white canvas, where everyone added their touch of color, making me the portrait I am today.

Fifty-two-year-old Scott "Beef" Bidwell was born and raised in Meadville, Pennsylvania. He was a former math teacher for Saegertown High School for twenty-four years. He also enjoys hunting and being in the great outdoors. Scott owned his own race team that raced around the tristate area for twenty-four years. He always enjoyed the support of his family, friends, and acquaintances. He now resides with his sister in Saegertown, Pennsylvania.